HOPE
WITHIN
HISTORY

Walter Brueggemann

John Knox Press
ATLANTA

Library of Congress Cataloging-in-Publication Data

Brueggemann, Walter.
  Hope within history.

  Bibliography: p.
  1. History (Theology) 2. Hope—Religious aspects—Christianity. I. Title.
  BR115.H5B74 1987   231.7'6   86-45353
  ISBN 0-8042-0918-9 (pbk.)

© copyright John Knox Press 1987
10 9 8 7 6 5 4 3 2
Printed in the United States of America
John Knox Press
Atlanta, Georgia 30365

Contents

To
HAROLD PETERS SCHULTZ
who hopes through his history

Introduction

The juxtaposition of "hope" and "history" articulates a central claim and a central problem of biblical faith. It also presents a central problem for our own context of believing and not believing. That juxtaposition is parallel to the christological formula of Chalcedon concerning Jesus as "truly God/truly human." *Hope in the true God* and *history of true humanity* constitute the central subject of the Bible. There is no doubt that the Bible narrates a genuine history of humanity with the reality of pain and amazement, of death and life. There is no doubt also that the Bible narrates the powerful hope-filled purposes of God which seem to operate and be visible in the processes of historical interaction. On the inscrutability of God's hope within history, the words of Joseph are poignant: "As for you, you meant evil against me; but God meant it for good, to bring it about that many people should be kept alive, as they are today" (Gen. 50:20). On the other hand, God's hope within history is proclaimed triumphantly:

1

The LORD of hosts has sworn:
"As I have planned,
 so shall it be,
and as I have purposed,
 so shall it stand,
that I will break the Assyrian in my land,
 and upon my mountains trample him under foot;
and his yoke shall depart from them,
 and his burden from their shoulder."
This is the purpose that is purposed
 concerning the whole earth;
and this is the hand that is stretched out
 over all the nations.
For the LORD of hosts has purposed,
 and who will annul it?
His hand is stretched out,
 and who will turn it back? (Isa. 14:24–27)

The tone of inscrutability and the mood of triumph both belong to the faith of the Bible, but they are noi easily held together. Perhaps the relation of biblical hope and history can be articulated only with textual and narrative specificity and not with any grand pattern. In any case, that is what is attempted here. The five discussions presented here seek to probe quite specific cases in which the hope of God is affirmed or discerned in the processes of historical interaction.

The word *history* has, of course, been problematic in recent scholarship, likely because modern Enlightenment understandings of history have been imposed on the biblical materials. The result has been that the Bible is pressed into the service of issues it does not appropriately address. By using the word *history* I mean simply the concrete interactions among persons, communities, and states which partake of hurt and healing. Thus I mean to bracket out the issues evoked by modern understandings, e.g., the problematic of *Geschichte* and *Historie.* Indeed I use the word only because I do not know what better word to use, though perhaps I should speak simply of "narrative events and narrated events."[1]

By *hope* I mean the resilient conviction that the processes of historical interaction are to be understood in relation to some overriding purpose that prevails in odd but uncompromising ways. Such a conviction of a prevailing purpose is expressed as "plan" in some of the most eloquent affirmations of the text:

> "For I know the plans I have for you, says the LORD, plans for welfare and not for evil, to give you a future and a hope. . . . I will be found by you, says the LORD, and I will restore your fortunes and gather you from all the nations and all the places where I have driven you, says the LORD, and I will bring you back to the place from which I sent you into exile." (Jer. 29:11–14)

> "For my thoughts are not your thoughts,
>   neither are your ways my ways, says the LORD.
> For as the heavens are higher than the earth,
>   so are my ways higher than your ways
>   and my thoughts than your thoughts." (Isa. 55:8–9)

The problem is how to speak both with seriousness of the reality of human experience and the bouyancy of these overriding claims which seem to preempt experience. Holding together the seriousness and the buoyancy cannot be done by a grand theory of predestination, but only through following the narrative of the community as it chooses and finds itself being chosen.[2]

The temptation among us is to split hope and history. As a result, we hold to a religious hope that is detached from the realities of the historical process, or we participate in a history which ends in despair because the process itself delivers no lasting victories for the participants. The problem is that, even though hope yields victories, history precludes enduring triumphs. Obviously such a split which yields both a historyless hope and a hopeless history is a betrayal of biblical faith. It is precisely the wonder and burden of the biblical texts that hope is relentlessly historical and history is cunningly hope-filled.

These five essays are attempts to exposit the peculiar juxtaposition of hope and history in the biblical text. They were originally presented as lectures in various places and were prepared without reference to each other. Only after their completion did it seem to me appropriate to place them together in a book, because they address a common and recurrent issue upon which I was reflecting during the time of their writing. Because the lectures were prepared for various contexts and settings, there is some tendency toward repetition, and at points some of the indicators of oral presentation persist. I assume, though, that neither of these factors gets in the way of the main point of the presentation.

The first two lectures, "The Exodus Narrative as Israel's Articulation of Faith Development" and "Righteousness as Power for Life," were presented at a conference on faith development initiated by James W. Fowler and included interaction with Fowler and Carol Gilligan. The two lectures are an attempt to respond seriously and critically to recent conversations in faith development and formation. It will be evident that my reading of the Bible both resonates with and has serious questions about faith development. The interface with Fowler has been important for me in my interpretation.

The third lecture, "Blessed Are the History-makers," has been used in several places. I wish especially to acknowledge its presentation as one of two lectures delivered as the 1984 Mendenhall Lectures at DePauw University, Greencastle, Indiana. That occasion was a university convocation in which honorary degrees were awarded to "history-makers," to less than famous persons who have devoted their lives to matters of justice, healing, and compassion in concrete and unheralded places. The persons honored there were embodiments of my themes of "history-making" and "prophetic destabilization." I am grateful to my friend, Fred Lamar, Campus Minister, and to Richard Rossiter, President, for their gracious hospitality to me. (My second Mendenhall lecture, "The Prophet as a Destabilizing Presence," has been printed in *The Pastor as Prophet* [ed. by Earl E. Shelp and Ronald H. Sunderland (New York: Pilgrim Press, 1985) 49–77].)

The fourth lecture, "Living Toward a Vision: Grief in the Midst of Technique," was presented through the Campus Ministry Program at Purdue University and subsequently to a national meeting of United Ministries in Education at Texas Christian University. The context of higher education in a scientific setting will illuminate the particular accents sounded there concerning hope and order in relation to the threat of technical reason.

The fifth lecture, "Will Our Faith Have Children?" was

presented as my inaugural lecture upon assuming an endowed chair at Eden Theological Seminary in 1983. It intends to articulate a paradigm for theological education in a church now deeply at odds with its cultural context, but the paradigm clearly has relevance beyond the specific locus of seminary education. It is reprinted in a slightly modified form from *Word and World* 3:3 (1983) 272–83. I am grateful to the editors for their permission to reprint it here.

In my judgment hope in history, hope through history, and hope beyond history (but not hope from history) will become increasingly pressing issues in the next decades for the American church. The two recent pastoral letters of the American Roman Catholic Bishops are a crucial sign that the Christian community in America is now readying itself for a major dispute with the dominant values of our culture that have run amok. Clearly, the dominant values of our culture, as they are embodied in economics, military policy, and sexuality (to name only the most obvious elements), are values of hopelessness. Equally clearly, much religion in America seduces one into a hope that is either privatistic or otherworldly. Before long we will have to face the issues of fidelity and enculturation and to insist on the cruciality of hope within a historical process that invites despair. I trust that these essays will be a useful, modest part of a conversation that is increasingly inescapable in the American church.

I have received encouragement from many quarters for these preparations and this publication. I express my thanks to Donna LaGrasso, who typed the manuscript, to Mary Swehla, a patient and generous secretary, and to Walter Sutton, of John Knox Press, who took the initiative with the manuscript. I am grateful to my colleague, Gail O'Day, who has critiqued the style and substance of the essays in important ways. Her input clarified for me some of my thinking.

I am delighted to dedicate this book to Harold Peters Schultz, my friend, colleague, and mentor in ministry and in theological education. It is through the gentleness, patience, passion, and generosity of Dr. Schultz that many of us at Eden Seminary have stronger faith, better theology, and more effective ministry. He would not articulate the themes of history and hope as I have done here, but he does embody them in remarkable ways. For a long time he has lived his history to the hilt, with joy and buoyancy and a wondrously innocent faith in the face of deep adversity. It is clear to many of us that his history is so buoyant because his hope is so powerful and relentless, so stayed on the living God who is both inscrutable and triumphant. These chapters are offered to him in thanksgiving and with affection for all that he embodies, for all that he provides for our theological community, and for all that he hopes so powerfully among us.

1

The Exodus Narrative as Israel's Articulation of Faith Development

In this chapter I intend to relate the claims of biblical narrative to current conversations concerning faith development.[1] Those conversations tend to proceed on largely formal grounds without attention to substantive issues of any particular faith affirmation.[2] My urging in this essay is that Israel's peculiar faith presentation (with particular reference to the normative narrative of the Exodus) requires that faith development be understood in a particular, concrete, radical, and transformative way. This insistence sets a biblical understanding apart from much of the conversation about faith development that attempts to be scientific and therefore substantively neutral. Clearly Israel's narrative is never, and never intends to be, substantively neutral, for Israel's faith is characteristically passionate in its partisan claims that concern both religious matters and social reality.

7

I

In Israel's primal narrative literature much is at stake,[3] not simply in the *original event* described but also in the anticipated impact of the *literature* which recurs again and again.[4] That is, transformative power is found not only in the Exodus event but also in the Exodus narrative,[5] not only in the encounter with Jesus but also in the encounter with the text about Jesus.[6] In a quite imprecise way this enduring power of the text must be what the tradition has meant by referring to this literature as "the live word of God." One does not need to be magical, supernaturalist, or superstitious to argue that this literature proceeds with a discernible power and intentionality that impinges upon and shatters all old descriptions of reality and invites one into a differently described reality. As a result of the character of this literature and its partisan claims, the conversation about faith development which is related to biblical faith should probably be transposed to a consideration of faith transformation. The Exodus narrative is not interested in development, but characteristically jars, assaults, and disorients so that development and growth are not adequate ways of speaking about changes that are wrought through discontinuity, displacement, and disjunction.

The literature on "stages of faith" tends to be a descriptive commentary on the plateau or placement of a person.[7] That is, the stage seeks to characterize a moment of equilibrium, but little attention is given to the difficult and largely inscrutable way of movement from one stage to another. That conservative predisposition to focus on equilibrium makes the descriptive enterprise essentially static. We may understand much about faith and personality from the perspective of stages of faith, but we are given no clue about the movement from stage to stage or about the religious dynamic that operates in the move.

By contrast, biblical literature focuses precisely on the move from one place or posture to another. This literature knows that the move is neither smooth nor explicable, but is characteristically disjunctive, painful, and hidden. Biblical literature focuses on the wrenching transitions, not on the stages. Perhaps that is true of all serious literature, especially literature that is cast as narrative and that claims to be disclosive, i.e., revelatory. Disclosure happens at points of disjunction, not in situations of equilibrium.[8] The Bible is concerned for transformation, communal and personal, which is disjunctive rather than developmental in any sustained or predictable way. It employs the dangerous language of narrative rather than the settled prose of description.[9] The biblical text, because it is a classic which continues to reveal,[10] intends not only to report on an ancient transformation but also to evoke and generate transformation in each new moment of its hearing.[11] Whereas development may yield classification, transformation resists such thematization.

My treatment here of Israel's interface with faith development will have a considerable social or sociological bent and may not be as singularly psychological, personal, or internal as is most often the case in current discussions of faith development. The "social construction of reality"[12] is crucial for psychological formation. While the relation of personal and social is surely dialectical, the social dimension appears to have priority and authority. Those who prefer to pursue a psychological articulation of faith development might resist the sociological inclination of the Exodus narrative by regarding it as primitive and lacking in psychological sophistication. Given that judgment, we would not expect this narrative literature to have the same insights that are available to us. Such a dismissive judgment, however, fails to appreciate the way in which this literature does indeed understand and articulate human personhood in subtle and discerning ways, even though the categories of articulation and discernment challenge the ways that have become normative in our culture.[13]

The Exodus literature mounts an argument that individual personhood is always a communal enterprise. Therefore the stages are never merely about *interiority* and yet are always about *interaction* in which the person is evoked, assaulted, and impinged upon in formative and transformative ways, depending on the other parties to the interaction. Such a view would correspond to the notion of covenant which many take to be the overriding metaphor of biblical faith.[14] The struggle to embrace covenantal modes of life is the story of faith development in Israel. That struggle is acute because covenantal practice is inevitably subversive of other modes of life. Maturation then is characteristically subversive.

II

In order to study the interface of the claims of the Bible and faith development, I will focus on the primal literature and the primal transformative memory of the Exodus. The text of Exodus 1—15 is a concrete historical memory, but it is now cast as a liturgical paradigm through which human experience is regularly processed.[15] By referring to this narrative as "liturgical," I refer to the public process carried on in a sustained and regular way in the community, whereby the community appropriates its normative memory and its governing metaphors. That process is not only recollective but also formative. That is, in the liturgical recital and enactment, Israel is "constructing" its own life and identity and permitting each new generation to appropriate it and to participate in its peculiar angle of vision.

According to this narrative Israel's understanding of human personhood comes through the experience and liturgic prism of liberation. Regularly it is to be asked by the child in time to come, "Why does my community perceive reality in this way and not in some other way?"[16] The answer to this question is given in the Exodus narrative. There is much we do not know about why this and no other narrative is presented as the governing paradigm in biblical faith. What we do know is that the Exodus narrative is an unquestioned, nonnegotiable given for any biblical understanding of human personhood. Given our concern for faith development, we may ask, what happens when human experience is redescribed, exposited, mediated, and embraced through this paradigmatic prism of liberation? What was intended to happen? What did happen? I propose three dimensions of this transformative redescription of life and personhood.

III

The first dimension of Israel's faith transformation is the *critique of ideology*. Each Israelite in every generation is immediately placed in the presence of the coercive power of Pharaoh: "The Egyptians treated us harshly" (Deut. 26:6). This is where Israel's story and self-identity begin. Every Israelite (adult or child) is personally thrust into a world of power politics and public reality.[17] We have no evidence that there is a prior stage of innocence, as if this community tried to protect its very young from the harsh realities of its skewed world.[18] Israel's self-identity is from the outset a public one. From the beginning, personal life is experienced as participation in and appropriation of the public realities of oppression and pain. Those realities are not just historically present; they are also given symbolic maximization through the liturgy which is person-shaping.

The Exodus narrative and literature offer a very particular reading of the public reality in which Israel is inevitably enmeshed. The narrative is fundamentally critical, a practice of what Ricoeur calls "suspicion"[19] or of what Schneidau calls "discontent."[20] The Bible is aware of a public world that is a network of *technological instruments* which are legitimated if not absolutized by religious and *mythopoetic ideology*. That imperial world is a stable, productive world that generates food and bestows life for all its adherents (cf. Gen. 47:13–26). Every individual person, along with the tribe and clan, is at the very outset placed in this world. One is not in a social vacuum, not even for a day. Life is not neutral or empty space. One has no innocence before one is in the world of the empire. One is from there and has one's being there. Israel concedes this, but it does not accept that locus as proper or normative. It practices a liturgy that intends to subvert that seemingly absolute shaping of social reality.

There is for Israel no "pre-empire" experience of social reality. There is no initial innocence or freedom. At the very beginning, the empire in all of its legitimated oppression is the context in which faith must be practiced and life must be lived. The empire is all-encompassing in shaping and defining life and reality.

Every Israelite person comes to know very early that one is claimed and identified in the empire and, for Hebrew slaves, one may guess, numbered and tattooed. From the beginning, Israelite identity is conflictual, for one knows without being told that *we do not belong to Pharaoh's world*.[21] That is an alien world and one must not be seduced there. The Egyptian-Canaanite technological-ideological lifeworld is not benign, neutral, or absolute. It is a contrivance of the dominant powers which are viewed in Israel both negatively and critically, because that social contrivance of imperial legitimacy is organized against justice, freedom, and humaneness, at least for the Israelite child receiving identity.

According to the Exodus credo, then, faith identity begins with the *critique of ideology*. From the beginning of one's life one is enmeshed and knows oneself to be so. As a member of this credo community, however, one is authoritatively summoned to break that enmeshment in whatever way one can. To articulate the matter of faith identity in this way may sound strangely like the old Christian orthodoxies that speak about the human predicament of enslavement to the power of sin. One is indeed enslaved, but in Israel's story the enslavement is not simply to a spiritual power. One is enslaved to a historically identifiable agent which has demonic force.[22] That imperial arrangement which enslaves Israel and which seems legitimated according to imperial ideology is not for one minute to be accepted as normative or deserving of either respect or obedience. Faith development consists in seeing the destructive power of the empire clearly and in having the freedom to act apart from and against it.

We may summarize Israel's characteristic critique of ideology in this way:

(1) The Israelite knows that he or she lives in a contrived world. Egyptian arrangements are not at all thought to be either absolute or worthy of trust and respect.

(2) The contrivance is not a matter of accident or indifference. It is quite intentionally designed to serve the special interests of some at the expense of others.

(3) Because this technological-ideological world is a contrivance and not a given, it may be undone and dismantled—*deconstructed*. The world may then be arranged in an alternative way if one has the courage and wits to do so.

(4) The agent of such dismantling, deconstruction, and delegitimation is *known by name—Yahweh*.[23] The Israelite

shaped by narrative recital is not a helpless, isolated victim but has an ally so powerful that the dismantling of the contrived empire is sure and can be counted on. That dismantling by Yahweh must be regularly and frequently replicated in liturgy, so that each new generation does not for a moment submit to the contrivance. As the liturgy legitimates a posture of refusal, so the posture results in various concrete acts of refusal, acts of freedom, which are derivative from the alternative paradigm offered in the liturgy on which the text is based. What Israel enacts regularly in the liturgy may occasionally be embraced in arenas of real historical danger and possibility.

Critique of ideology as a first step in faith development does not easily fit into any growth or developmental model because it is disjunctive. It is better understood as liberationist or transformative rather than developmental. The Israelite person at first glance knows himself or herself *to be a creature enmeshed but nonetheless destined for freedom,* as is confirmed in the counterparadigm. This set of affirmations is linked to the conviction that the world as is is under criticism and will not be the world that is sure to come. In this way the Exodus narrative describes not only "a mighty deed of God in history" but also a clue to a specific notion of human personality which is transformative and redescriptive.

The actual material of the critique of ideology is not extensive. I cite three texts, all of which are narrative rather than rational analysis. Israel's imagined world is a world created by narrative. It is precisely the story of the Exodus that intends to break the system.[24]

(1) In Exodus 1:2–14 and 5:7–9, 17–19 we are given policy statements in the mouth of Pharaoh which purport to be actual governmental decrees. It is clear that no government ever actually issued a decree that was as crass as the textual wording, for these purported decrees show that Pharaoh is explicitly planning and insisting upon harshness, inhumaneness, and exploitation. No authority is ever that explicit, shameless, or candid. More likely this is not what Pharaoh said, but rather is Israel's polemical narrative

interpretation of imperial policies.[25] This partisan rendering of the imperial decree is thus not a factual report but a critique from the perspective of the victims. The alleged report is not what the Egyptians said but what the Israelites must hear if the system is to be "unmasked" and seen for its real intent. The narrative itself does not invite us to a scientific critique, because it is itself a critique, reporting what is in fact operative in the empire, if we can turn our eyes away from the ideology that tries to conceal the true state of affairs. Each new generation, as it participates in this narrative, learns how to make and engages in this social criticism of established power. The capacity and the freedom for such criticism are central to faith maturation in Israel's self-understanding.

The purpose of the narrative, generation after generation, is to enhance faith formation in a conflictual, disjunctive way. The Egyptian program here enunciated becomes a model for every social setting which is judged by Israel to fall short of covenantal humaneness. The Israelite is given an identity of critical awareness and the boldness to begin to think through alternatives that lie outside the legitimated structure which is now dramatized as inadequate and tentative.

(2) In the plague narratives of Exodus 6—10, which are repetitious and highly stylized, the dismantling critique is intensified. The narrative dramatizes the power struggle between Moses and the "wise men,"[26] between Yahweh and Pharaoh. The narrative mounts in intensity until in 8:18 it is clear that Pharaoh has failed and warrants no further allegiance. In 11:7 the conclusion is drawn which is decisive for the narrative and decisive for all coming generations whose faith is formed through this narrative: "Yahweh makes a distinction between the Egyptians and Israel." Israelites are certainly not to be like the Egyptians, exploitative of others, but they also are not intended to be victims of such a system. Thus identity has to do with faith and life lived *outside the imperial system* in a zone of freedom and justice. This is faith formation which nurtures persons to live outside the dominant system with the courage and imagination to construct countersystems of reality.[27]

(3) A third narrative of criticism is in Genesis 47:13—21. This text is a rather surprisingly sober rendition of the origin of this

entrapment in ideology. The narrative answers the question, "If this Egyptian enmeshment is not as we are supposed to live, how and why did we arrive at this place?" One cannot move out of such a system unless one understands critically how it was that there was a move into it.

The answer begins with a monopoly of food. As the hungry ones came for food:

(a) In the first year, their *money* was taken (vs. 14).
(b) Then their *cattle* were taken (vs. 17).
(c) In the next year their *land* was taken, and their *bodies,* and they became slaves (vss. 18–19), for they said, "Why should we die?"

The conclusion is drawn in verse 21: "As for the people, he made slaves of them from one end of Egypt to the other." This text is not simply a report. It is a mighty narrative protest against the state monopoly of goods and the monopoly of "the means of production." The purpose of the text is to assault the imperial system that reduces some to bondage, for the monopoly of food and life advantage is ill-gotten, illegal, and immoral. The present power arrangements in the empire are under judgment because they are obtained at the price of freedom and justice.

We might wish for a more scientific analysis, but this community does its serious critique in narrative form. Israel knows that the dominant ideology will be destroyed by the proper telling of the story. That is why ancient Israel "loved to tell the story" and why "those who knew it best seemed hungering and thirsting to hear it like the rest." The retelling of the text is to remember who we are. The mode of story is the only way to get at the concreteness of hurt that will lead to action. The story both discloses how Israel was enslaved and mediates the power to undertake transformative, liberating action.

The practice of faith formation embodied in these narratives offers to every man, woman, and child access to the fundamental shaping event in Israel.[28] No child is too young and no adult is too well situated not to recognize that this is the fundamental articulation of Israel's reality. Faith, read in this context, is the unblushing and unblinking assertion that the cards are unjustly stacked in the empire, and there is the unshakable conviction of freedom and justice to come which requires a dismantling of the imperial world. The imperial world is indeed a contrived and illegitimate arrangement, and it cannot last. The whole liturgic life of Israel is an act of "deconstruction."[29]

IV

A second, closely related element in Israel's faith formation is the *public processing of pain*. Reinhold Niebuhr, in one of his great aphorisms, observed that one never willingly gives up power. Certainly Pharaoh does not. Therefore a move out of Egyptian enmeshment is not happy or congenial. The issue must be forced from underneath. The victims of the enmeshment must make the first move, but precisely because they are victims, they cannot make such a move. They are paralyzed, bought off, or intimidated through a carefully nurtured symbiotic relationship of dependency upon the system.[30] This Exodus narrative, however, asserts a remarkable recognition. Subservience is what we would expect . . . but it is not so in Israel. The purpose of the social criticism is to create a basis for a bold move of disengagement.

(1) Social criticism and exposure of the dominant ideology are important. They, however, only give insight, and insight never liberated anyone. They do not give power or authority to make a move of withdrawal or delegitimation. Such power and authority to move in the face of imperial definitions of reality come from *the public processing of pain*. By "public processing" I refer to an intentional and communal act of expressing grievance which is unheard of and risky under such an absolutist regime. The faith-forming story has its second phase, "and we cried out." Think what a subversive, revolutionary move that is! It is not revolutionary to experience pain. The regime does not deny the reality of pain. Or, if one notices the pain, one must not credit it for much. Simply to notice the pain, though, is not the same as public processing. As long as persons experience their pain privately and in isolation, no social power is generated. That is why every regime

has a law against assembly. When there is a meeting, there is a social anger which generates risky, passionate social power. In Israel such a meeting might have been:

(a) a political meeting of protest,
(b) the lodging of a formal protest in court, according to all proper procedure, or
(c) a liturgical act of stylized assault.[31]

It could have been any of these, or all of these. The reason it could have been all of these is that the oppressed communities do not have everything slotted. A meeting in court thus can become a liturgical moment. A liturgical moment can become a political protest. The rulers of the dominant ideology want to categorize such meetings because that makes for control. The dominant class does not want liturgy to spill over into political discourse. That is why the "spiritual leader" is to keep clear of political questions. How *un*-Israelite!

In any case, this moment of outcry in Israel is a moment of "going public" in an irreversible act of civil disobedience.[32] The outcry is an announcement for all to notice that the peasants would no longer conform to the system, silently meet production quotas, and go home at night exhausted. The outcry is an announcement that Israel would no longer bow before the imperial ideology, because the slaves had noticed that the ideology did not square with the reality of pain in their own lives which no amount of ideology could lead them to deny. The outcry is an announcement that the peasants would no longer have their lives defined by the dominant *technology*. They would no longer bow before the *ideology* offered by the ruling class. The "withdrawal" is surely liturgical, political, economic, psychological—the end of the "known world" of Egypt.[33]

Such an action is unheard of in the ancient world. It is a withdrawal from the "sacred canopy,"[34] a disengagement from the only known world, a rejection of the rules of the game, a denial of the theodicy sponsored by the system.[35] The cry of pain begins the formation of a countercommunity around an alternative perception of reality. The only source of such a countercommunity is to trust one's pain and to trust the pain of one's neighbor which is very much like our own.

(2) The public processing of pain, however, is not only a bold articulation. As Israel tells its faith-forming narrative, the pain is received, resolved, and honored by Yahweh, the Lord of the Exodus: "Yahweh heard our cry, knew our condition, saw our affliction, and came down to save." That reception and response by Yahweh also belongs to the narrative, and without it the narrative would collapse.

(a) This response on the part of Yahweh is a surprise. The first actor in the story does not know of Yahweh ahead of time. It does not say Israel cried out "to him." The cry was not addressed to Yahweh or to anyone, but nonetheless it evoked Yahweh's answer. Faith formation in Israel affirms that the cry of pain and oppression does not occur against an empty, indifferent sky. Thus Yahweh's appearance in the narrative, while a great surprise, is the decisive factor.

(b) It may seem strange to include such a primitive theological reference in an analysis of faith formation, but that is precisely the point. The narrative cannot be told without this reference. Faith cannot be formed without Yahweh. Israel's narrative does not glorify pain. It has no interest in autonomous individuals, heroic or otherwise, questing about for freedom. Faith formation is faith in this God evoked in this community which lies outside the system. Faith formation cannot be reported simply as a formal grid but only as a substantive affirmation vis-à-vis this God like whom there is no other in any grid (Exod. 15:11). Faith formation means to convey the uniqueness of Yahweh and hence the distinctiveness of Israel.[36] Take this agent, Yahweh, out of the narrative and there is no faith formation. For Israel, faith formation must have an explicit theological element that cannot be reduced or translated into more general religious or formal terms.

(c) Yahweh's appearance may be a surprise to the slave community. It may be an oddity for careful analysis. Clearly, however, Yahweh is now for all time a strategic character in the story.[37] Israel's narrative, revolutionary as it is, asserts that the decisive source of life is fully outside the regnant system. The system therefore is never the solution, for only Yahweh is finally the solution to the problem of identity and of oppression.

There is a liberating agent outside the system who turns out to be reliable and powerful. First, though, the cry is made without reference to an agent, just a profound yearning and desperate hopeful pain with no assurance of being heard.[38] That is, the *relinquishment of system* comes before the *embrace of the Holy One*. The rock bottom of faith formation then is recognition of and communal articulation of the pain that belongs inevitably to the social process where our faith persons are both evoked and crushed.

The crucial hinge in this faith formation is the *pivotal power of pain*.[39] That is the Bible's most dangerous insight and the one it may best contribute to our current discussion concerning faith and culture. Such an accent tells against all growth psychologies and, indeed, against all ideologies which function by cover-up, whitewash, and denial. It is precisely the public processing of pain that permits and evokes redescription which gives a chance for newness.

The relationship between our first two points, the critique of ideology and the public processing of pain, is not clear. One cannot be sure whether the notice of pain *results from or energizes* the critique of ideology. The two elements are dialectical; each reinforces or evokes the other. My sociological inclination is that critique of ideology comes first. That is, the identification and exposé of false forms of social reality permit one to notice the pain. This is the way the narrative is told in ancient Israel. Moses' killing of the Eyptian (Exod. 2:11–15) is an act of criticism which sets the scene for the public cry of 2:23–25. It takes such a bold inexplicable act to mobilize a public protest.

Moses' act is indeed an act of critique, for the text says, "He went out and saw his people and looked on their burdens. And he saw an Egyptian beating a Hebrew, one of his people. He looked this way and that, and seeing no one, he killed the Egyptian, and hid him in the sand" (Exod. 2:11–12, author's translation). The result of Moses' violent act was the public act of Israel in voicing the deep pain that had been systematized by the empire, domesticated by the mythology, and regarded as legitimate and beyond criticism. It is only a break in the regime, the death of Pharaoh, that lets Israel exercise its pain, for the text says, "In the course of those many days the king of Egypt died. And the people of Israel groaned under their bondage" (2:23). That act of pain is Israel's remarkably subversive assertion. It is an act of defiance and protest. It is also an act of hope. In that moment of public process, the calculus is changed for Israel. It is changed in heaven, for Yahweh is moved out of the divine council in order to care. It is changed on earth, for Pharaoh is now placed deeply under assault. The act of pain started the whole movement which leads to new Israel.

If this narrative enactment is taken as an articulation of faith formation, it is an invitation to each new generation in this community to take this reading of reality as normative. To be an Israelite means to read social reality through the legitimacy and primacy of pain. It permits no ideology to cover over the pain which is judged to be the crucial element in the reality of the community and, indeed, in the reality of the person.[40]

V

The third element in this story which relates to faith formation is that the public outcry and processing of pain in Israel leads to *the release of new social imagination.* The cry takes the lid off Israel's hope-filled imagination. The Exodus event and the resilient power of the Exodus narrative have enabled many generations of people to say, "It's our turn now, and we have not had a turn in a long time."[41] The question always asked of the ones liberated in their pain is, "What will you do with your time?" Juices are set free which enable those who have not hoped for a long time to hope, those who have not imagined for a long time to imagine. Over a long period of containment, all parties begin to think that the way it is now is the only way it could be. The managers of the ideology carefully nurture such a view. After a while the oppressed feebly and helplessly but willingly begin to accept that view.

When the cry comes to voice, however, there is a new ability, courage, and will to hope, imagine, design, and implement alternative scenarios of how it could be. The next period of Israel's faith formation is the practice of a social imagination of a new kind. I stress *social*, for in Israel it is never a covetous, autonomous, private imagination but always a new way to shape the community.⁴² This act of social imagination is always under assault from alternative forms which want to privatize and reduce this imagination. The Pharaohs of the world encourage privatization, for that leads to abdication and resignation in the public arena. Privatization of imagination permits conformity in public adminis-tration. The articulation of this release of social imagination is evident in many aspects, of which we will consider three.

(1) The first evidence of social imagination is evidenced in *The Song of Miriam/Song of Moses* (Exod. 15:1–18, 21).⁴³ It might be termed a victory song, but I take it as a liturgic enactment of a changed social situation, of a transformed sense of reality, and an assertion of a new sense of freedom. For what is a victory song other than the celebration that the powers of enslavement have been terminated? This is the liturgic moment when the lament of 2:23–25 is changed into dance, song, and celebration, an act of freedom and self-assertion unrestrained by the power of Egyptian ideology.⁴⁴

The substance of the song is that our God is stronger, incomparably stronger than your god. It follows that our mode of reality is no longer controlled and administered by your mode of reality. In this poetic act Israel first tells an alternative story, enacts an alternative reality, envisions a different shaping of life. Yet the mode is as important as the substance. This is indeed a "hoedown," not only in the sense of dance but also in the sense of a work stoppage, acting freely in someone else's world without obeying. Perhaps for the brickyards, it should be called a "hod-down." I submit that it is liturgy because scenarios must be tried in the safety of the community before one can go public in a hostile arena. So a *ritual defiance* occurs before there is any *public defiance*.⁴⁵ This is experimentation which Wilder calls "guerilla theater,"⁴⁶ in which the dismantling of the old assumptive world is under way.

(2) The first act is liturgic; the second act is political. They made their way to Sinai where they publicly articulated another way of reality. What they did was change gods. As Martin Buber has seen, they rejected the kingship of Pharaoh as they received and affirmed

the kingship of Yahweh (Exod. 19:4–6).[47] The alternative of Sinai is not individualistic anarchy in which "every one does what is right in his or her own eyes" (cf. Judg. 21:25). Rather there is the forming of a new political entity which provides standing ground for rejecting the old political realities of Pharaoh and Egypt.

Before Mendenhall[48] and Gottwald,[49] Buber saw that this act is an allegiance to the kingdom of God. In biblical faith, both Old and New Testaments, "kingdom of God" is the core metaphor for a new social imagination.[50] Think what a remarkable juxtaposition of terms it is to say "kingdom of God." The word "God" conventionally refers to what is awesome, other, transcendent, spiritual. The term "kingdom" refers to power as it is organized to make a difference in the real world. The full phrase, "kingdom of God," thus speaks about a concentration of power and authority *like* the kingdom of Egypt and yet utterly *unlike* it, a social construction of reality that judges and critiques every other social construction of power and authority. At Mount Sinai these slaves with their hoedowns enter into a new mode of life with dreams of freedom and justice and with new rules of obedience which are stringent and demanding. There they vow that they shall be utterly free in this relationship, that they will never again submit to old ideological patterns of control.

In the New Testament the metaphor, "kingdom of God," stands at the center of the social imagination of Jesus. His parables are articulations of the kingdom, clearly in metaphorical modes. His miracles are enactments of the kingdom which are rightly perceived by his opposition as subversive assaults on the rulers of this age. The parabolic articulation of these teachings is important, because it is the only way that the imaginative project can keep from becoming flattened into a new system of coercion and exploitation.

(3) The social imagination of liberated Israel is not only a *liturgic* act (The Song of Moses) or a *political* act (of changing sovereigns at Sinai). It is also a *legislative* act. Social imagination cannot forever stay impressionistic and fanciful. It may begin in dreams, but it leads to acts of public shaping derived from the dreams. Israel could begin by a new joyous dance, but then it had to translate the power and intention of the dance into concrete economic and political terms. This is the work of torah.

Torah is practice and implementation of social imagination,[51] a dream of how to order life in new modes, faithful to the gift of the Exodus. One example of such social imagination which seeks *to make God's covenanting kingdom concrete* is the tradition of Deuteronomy.[52] Deuteronomy can be treated simply as legislation. It is, however, much more a scenario into an alternative shaping of human life. That was the insight of von Rad when he termed it "preached law," as much preaching as legislation.[53] A central construct of Deuteronomy is the contrast between *Israel covenanted in the wilderness,* where Israel relies on God, and *Canaanites in the land,* where the techniques of exploitative religion and oppressive politics are said to pertain. No doubt this is in part an imaginative construct in which the contrast is sharpened to urge the alternative. As Deuteronomy tells it, these seem like well-ordered and discrete spheres, separating land and wilderness, distinguishing the governance of Yahweh the God of Israel from that of the gods of Canaan.

Deuteronomy, however, makes the extraordinarily venturesome suggestion: the fertile land does not need to be ordered in Canaanite ways. The land can be ordered in covenantal ways according to the rule of Yahweh the Lord of the covenant. The legal provisions of this torah constitute an alternative proposal:[54]

(a) a year of release which would seem to undermine all conventional economics (Deut. 15:1–11);
(b) a prophetic word instead of religious technique (18:9–22);
(c) a king, but one who merely reads the torah (17:14–20);
(d) cities of refuge to curb unauthorized violence (19:1–10);
(e) collateral for loans returned to the poor at night (24:10–13);
(f) hospitality for runaway slaves (23:15–16);
(g) payments of wages to the poor on the day earned, to prevent exploitative use of the money belonging to another (24:14–15).

As Belo has discerned,[55] there is also an impetus for laws which militate against such a liberated view of society and which contradict the vision of Jubilee.[56] Nevertheless there are many other laws like those above that might be cited in support of the vision of a liberated community. The kingdom of God is a guiding metaphor out of which bold, concrete decisions are made, even if the vision does not totally govern the imagination of Israel.

VI

In summary, I suggest that the dynamic of faith from the perspective of the Exodus narrative always consists in these three moves:

(1) Expression of a dangerous *critique of ideology* which has shaped personhood according to dominant myths that reflect dominant social interests. Any theory of development which does not face this fact of oppressive ideology seems to me to be excessively innocent and domesticated.

(2) Articulation of and *embrace of the pain* which the dominant myths have tried to deny and cover over. All the way from the cry in Egypt to a theology of the cross, this tradition has affirmed that fresh and mature faith has been strangely given in the disjunctions which are costly.

(3) *Practice of social imagination,* authorized and energized by public processing of pain, is an act of dangerous subversion but also an act of concrete hope.

As is always the case with Jewishness, there is something angular and not very accommodating about these claims. The focus is not on the "stage" but on the *move* from one point to another. The Old Testament is not terribly interested in the equilibrium to be found in any particular moment but instead comes to voice at the breakpoints.[57] This movement of personality is ongoing in its dynamic, because old forms of social imagination tend to become new modes of oppressive ideology in need of critique. I do not believe this is "cyclical," but Israel does know that one must return again and again to the primal texts (Exodus) and the root metaphors (covenant, kingdom) in order to be free for new futures and new hopes.

Three elements in my argument seem to distance this portrayal from current discussions of faith development.

(1) The moves discerned here have *a specific theological reference*. That is, Yahweh is an active agent. The narrative concerns a specific God with a particular name and a particular history in the world. One cannot, in this narrative, work with empty, formal categories but must presume the God of Israel who

(a) is allied against the empire,
(b) intervenes for the lowly ones, and
(c) invites Israel to a new future shaped like the kingdom of God.

Reference to this God is an unavoidable part of Israel's discernment. Any presentation of Israel's notion of faith which denies this focus is inadequate.

(2) The focus here has been on the function of speech, rhetoric, and imagination, i.e., *the life of symbolization in the community*. Perhaps the reason for this may be that our subject has been *texts* rather than persons, so I have had to turn to these matters. Beyond that, it is clear that concrete symbols which grew out of specific experience (as distinct from universal myths) are in fact formative and evocative of faith in personal experience and in community experience. Too much discussion of faith development misses out on this creative, artistic dimension of faith formation which tends to view language as technical and descriptive rather than noticing the linguistic vehicles for evocation. The symbolization in Israel around Exodus/Sinai/land/torah is foundational for Israelite personhood. If one pays attention to symbolization, then one must talk about public discourse and the decisive shaping of faith done by a particular historical community. The convergence of *symbolization—text—community* is suggestive of what the Old Testament may have to contribute to our study of faith development.

(3) My analysis may appear to be excessively sociological in a field that has tended to be psychological. Such an emphasis reflects a conviction about the formative power of the community on the person, but, more specifically, the Israelite sense of the primacy of the community can scarcely be doubted. It is indeed community which evokes, permits, and legitimizes persons of faith.

This argument about faith development, then, may sound

strange for reasons of theological *referent,* because of the stress on *symbolization* and because of the *primacy of the sociological.* Nonetheless, I believe it is a helpful way of speaking of faith formation. This way of discerning reality is peculiarly Israelite and is intimately tied to these particular texts. Yet these texts hold that every process of transformation and genuine faith, in whatever social context, if rightly perceived, moves in this fashion. This is Israel's reading of all reality, not only its own (cf. Amos 9:7).

Faith formation is a process of choosing gods, as did the peasants with Deborah (Judg. 5:8), as did Joshua and his house (Josh. 24:14–15). In choosing this new God who is dangerously jealous and radically compassionate, the peasant community always found it had also chosen *a new mode of social existence* along with the *new God.* This God may not be chosen apart from a particular social existence.

2

Righteousness as Power for Life

Out of the traditions of Moses I have tried to argue that faith transformation may be understood in three moves:

(1) critique of the dominant theology,
(2) public embrace of pain as alternative to the dominant ideology, and
(3) release of social imagination.[1]

In this chapter the same categories of analysis are used in another way to do two related things, a study of righteousness as a motif in faith development and a study of righteousness in the book of Isaiah.

I

First, I want to consider the *Old Testament meaning of righteousness* as it may relate to faith formation. The word "righteousness" *(ṣaddîq, ṣedāqāh)* is of course a word that can be used in a variety of ways.[2] I will indicate here four dimensions which may be drawn together.

(1) Righteousness is peculiarly and decisively a *mark of God's godness*. God is the one who does righteousness (cf. Mic. 6:5) and who is righteous (cf. Jer. 12:1). In the biblical tradition it is out of the righteousness of God that Jesus can speak of the new righteousness (Matt. 5:17–20) and Paul can speak of the righteousness of faith (Rom. 10:1–4). When assigned to human persons, it is always reflective of and derivative of the righteousness of God. Its usage for creatures is an affirmation that all of life is understood in reference to God, i.e., theonomously.[3] Human persons are righteous insofar as they accept their destiny as God's responsive creatures.

(2) Righteousness is (no doubt more popularly) a *moral category*, dealing with full and utter obedience, with a social conscience. Kurt Galling has identified a series of texts which catalog dimensions of this understanding, culminating in Job 31, for it is Job who is indeed the fully righteous man.[4] Righteousness as a human characterization is a shaping of human life according to God's intent and even according to God's person. It is a quality of ethical "imitation."

(3) Righteousness marks one as *intensely social and communal*, concerned for the quality and character of human interaction (Ps. 112:3, 6, 9). The conventional stereotype of righteousness as personal purity or integrity misses the point because the term is characteristically used in tandem with "justice."

(4) Righteousness is characteristically *promissory, anticipatory, and eschatological*. Such a notion is under no illusion about the character of things as they are, but it is never willing to settle for how the world is presently arranged. That is, the righteous one is capable of hope, intensely believes that things can and will be different from the way they now are, and boldly acts on that basis and toward that hope.

All of these elements together may be summarized in the statement that righteousness is the *power to give life*. God is known as the one who can give life. Others who derive strength, gifts, and authority from God may also be endowed with the power to give life. That is an enormous claim to make for any human creature. Life-giving power is *theonomous,* for the power to give life belongs peculiarly to God and only derivatively to anyone else. It is *social,* for the giving of life is always to another, never securing it for oneself, which we cannot do, for life is always and must be gift. It is *material,* for the Bible knows that the gift of life consists in the turf, the wherewithal, and the power to choose one's way and shape one's future.

We may marvel at this power to give life, for we should not take it as a notion that is too easy or too obvious. Clearly, to speak of the power to give life is to speak in a poetic, metaphorical way which cannot be contained in a scientific or technical assertion. For how does one give life? We do not know. We know we cannot invent it. We do have the sense that something inscrutable, beyond us, is at work. Also we do not blink from lodging that inscrutability in some sense of the holy, the mysterious, the other, which in the biblical tradition we refer to as the sovereignty of God. Accounts of life-giving are always presented in narrative, because only narrative brings to expression the hidden powerful reality of life-giving.

A biblical notion of righteousness is useful for a study of faith development, for it insists that faith development is not a set of empty, formal categories, but is a substantive matter that can be analyzed according to some identifiable if not measurable categories. The "more developed" faith is

> *more faithfully theonomous,* more referred to God, i.e., informed by and accountable to the holy beyond our containment; not only accountable but also graced by energy, power, and authority.

> *more intentionally addressed to the community,* understanding that life is public. Personal destiny is at issue in the well-being of the neighbor, so the individualistic model of "hero" is hardly applicable. Maturity entails care for the neighbor.

> *more trustingly open to the future,* convinced that a community more life-giving than the one we have is promised and is sure to

be given. That future which is sure stands under the metaphor "kingdom of God."[5] This metaphor requires and permits one to be genuinely critical of all present communities, no matter how much they are regarded as absolute and beyond criticism. This future toward which one is to be open is not a blur. It is intentional and defined in a concrete though elusive way, marked by the *narratives* of deliverance and blessing in this community. The narratives of the Bible characteristically can say, "The coming kingdom is like. . . ."

more responsibly integrated into a moral life, which completely embraces the best ethical and legal traditions, takes them seriously and embodies them, and then moves beyond them to more radical obedience, not to a kind of transcendence which nullifies and supersedes obedience but to one which does neighborliness in extreme ways.

Transformation in faith is the assertion that one may be given the power to give life, to receive that gift and act out of it. One may speak about *the gift of lifepower* in various metaphors: legal (justification, acquittal), prophetic (liberation), priestly (atonement), royal (enthroned). Whatever metaphor we prefer, it is clear that to practice righteousness is to make the power of death less powerful, less attractive, and less seductive. One need not approach the neighbor under the threat of death or as a threat of death. Our theme then is the forming of the righteous person in a community of righteousness, responsive to God and attentive to neighbor.

II

The second matter under consideration is the shape and claims of the *book of Isaiah;* specifically we will consider the ways in which righteousness as norm and substance is understood and presented in that literature. In order to do that, some preliminary comments on the book of Isaiah are in order. The book of Isaiah has had a long, complicated redactional history. The critical consensus to which I subscribe is as follows:

Isaiah 1—39. The First Isaiah is largely from the eighth-century Isaiah in Jerusalem and is concerned with the Assyrian crisis and the jeopardy of Jerusalem.

Isaiah 40—55. Second Isaiah, dated 540 B.C.E., is addressed to Jews exiled under Babylon and announces that homecoming is possible and soon to be accomplished due to the rise of Cyrus the Persian who is presented as God's liberating Messiah.

Isaiah 56—66. A Third Isaiah, dated around 500 B.C.E., is addressed to Jews who have returned home to Jerusalem and must rebuild the ruined city on the basis of new hopes. Hanson[6] and Achtemeier[7] have urged that this community is one opposed to the established powers of the priesthood, and so is open to radical transformation in the community.

On the whole, Isaiah study has treated these three pieces of literature as quite distinct literary-theological efforts, almost as though they are quite independent entities which only accidentally happen to be in the same scroll. Only quite recently Brevard Childs[8] and Ronald Clements[9] have urged that, due to the canonical shape of the literature, we must take seriously the juxtaposition of these literary elements, to see how the present shape of the literature is important. The literary arrangement is not accidental, but is theologically intentional.

Childs and Clements make the proposal around the single juxtaposition of 1—39 and 40—66 without greater refinement. Second Isaiah repeatedly speaks of "former things" that are to be forgotten and "new things" which are now being wrought by God (cf. 42:9; 43:9, 16–19; 44:6–8; 45:9–13, 20–21; 46:9–11). Childs and Clements urge that the "new things" are in fact all *the promises of God* and the "former things" now to be forgotten are *the punishments and judgments* of God which have come to fruition.[10] Thus the theme of "old thing/new thing" is transposed into *judgment of God/promise of God,* and this is correlated with First Isaiah as *the old thing of judgment* and with Second-Third Isaiah as *the new thing of promise.* The interrelations of the parts of Isaiah get handled in terms of *judgment and promise.*

Two criticisms may be made against this view, without taking up the more comprehensive issue of canon criticism. First, Childs and Clements offer a somewhat static presentation which still offers no clue about why this literature is placed this way, i.e., what experiential dynamic caused the move from the one to the other to be made. Second, that analysis ignores Third Isaiah and reduces the three parts to a single juxtaposition, against the critical consensus. Yet one must ask whether Third Isaiah does not in fact offer a third element, i.e., a second move. On these two issues, a socio-experiential dynamic and a threefold set, I have proposed that the book of Isaiah be understood in a broad sweep in this way:

> *Isaiah 1—39* as a *critique of ideology,* showing why Israel is under such acute judgment.

> *Isaiah 40—55* as an *embrace of pain,* the processing of Israel's hurt and displacement, suggesting that suffering is a new vocation that is to be embraced by Israel.

> *Isaiah 56—66* as the *unleashing of social imagination* toward a new Jerusalem, made possible only because the pain has been embraced and processed, so that a new scenario is possible.[11]

Thus, I propose to understand the book of Isaiah in the same terms I used to explore the Moses traditions in chapter 1. Such an analysis is inevitably somewhat reductionist, but it may be a way to think seriously about a new paradigm for understanding the claims of the entire corpus.

The book of Isaiah thus may be considered as a presentation of *the theme of righteousness,* with sufficient scope for something of a longitudinal study. In doing that I propose to consider the interface between *righteousness as the power to give life*[12] and *the three parts of Isaiah* as critique of ideology, embrace of pain, and release of social imagination. I suggest that the book of Isaiah provides materials out of which we can think how it is that faith transformation is wrought and to what purpose. My hope in investigating these very large themes together is to suggest:

(1) If we keep our eye on *righteousness,* we will learn something about faith development/transformation.

(2) The development of the book of Isaiah is something of an analogue for the development of faith in the community gathered around the text as it matures in its embrace and practice of God's righteousness.

III

First Isaiah as a critique of ideology. In this material, righteousness functions as a critical principle to expose and condemn social practice, a form of faith in which there is no power for life because the practice violates God's intentions. Righteousness makes clear that the society here addressed by Isaiah is a processor and agent of death (cf. Isa. 28:14–18). Death may finally come at the hands of the Assyrians, but in fact it comes because the holy God will not forever accept such an incongruity between God's will and the social result in Israel.[13] The thrust of Isaiah 1—39 in its main lines, therefore, is harsh and relentless because it exposes the systemic self-deception of the royal-temple establishment, which in the ancient world is the rough equivalent of the military-industrial complex. If we are to speak about the faith development in Jerusalem which is here assaulted by the prophetic poet, it is a faith reduced to ideology, a symbolization of life without any self-critical capacity, in which religion serves simply to legitimate the crassest vested interests that are operative. While the public order is ordained to justice and righteousness (9:7), in fact justice and righteousness are completely absent (5:7). In this diverse and complex literature of First Isaiah, we may identify five elements in the use of righteousness.

(1) Only once (5:16) is our term related directly to God:

> But the LORD of hosts is exalted in justice,
>   and the Holy God shows himself holy in righteousness.

This is a rather remarkable statement. In Isaiah, as in Amos, the word pair "righteousness/justice" is often used to speak about the quality of equity and humaneness to be practiced in society.[14] But the grammar of 5:16 affirms that through this social practice, God is caused to be holy. The holiness of God is at issue in the social practice of righteousness. By this sweeping theonomous note, the prophet goes far in asserting that righteousness is not simply an ethical norm. A social practice of righteousness impinges upon the character of God. The context serves to show that, as God is elevated by such a shape of society, so righteousness also serves to crush human arrogance and pride. That is, righteousness serves to restore a proper interaction between God and humankind which is surely perverted by uncriticized ideology. Restoration of the covenant between Yahweh and Israel depends on a proper social practice.

(2) In two passages (28:17 and 33:15) righteousness is laid out as the norm for viable communal life. The first of these occurs in a poem of intricate construction usually assigned to Isaiah (28:14–22). This poem begins at verse 14, and it ends at verse 22 with a warning against those who scoff at God's sovereignty. In another metaphor, in verses 15, 18, Israel is said to have made a "covenant with death."[15] The one who scoffs at God, who ignores God's sovereignty, who engages in self-serving ideology, is bound for death, for life is linked to righteousness.[16]

In 28:17, the norm is asserted:

> "And I will make justice the line,
>   and righteousness the plummet;
>   and hail will sweep away the refuge of lies,
>   and waters will overwhelm the shelter."

"Refuge" and "shelter" refer to the self-serving ideology that fails both to disclaim the power of death and to care about the power for life. God's sovereignty requires attention to the power for life. Whoever does not give that attention is under threat.

The same normative character of God's righteous will is asserted in 33:15. It is reported in verse 14 that sinners are afraid, that the godless are seized by trembling. These categories are not to be understood in moralistic terms, but refer to living life and arranging royal "truth" in self-serving ways. An alternative is offered in verses 15–16:

> He who walks righteously and speaks uprightly,
>   who despises the gain of oppressions,
>   who shakes his hands, lest they hold a bribe,

> who stops his ears from hearing of bloodshed,
> and shuts his eyes from looking upon evil,
> he will dwell in the heights; . . .
> his bread will be given him, his water will be sure.

The "developed" person is one who does not engage in collusion to disrupt the community and exploit the helpless.

(3) On the basis of *the holiness of God* and *the ethical norm of righteousness*, we may consider uses of righteousness which are central to First Isaiah, texts which state Yahweh's quarrel with Israel for having arranged life against righteousness. The issues are characteristically public and social. Indeed, Israel could not think in private or personalistic ways about faith or faith formation. Isaiah 5:7 is a famous play on words:

> he looked for *justice* [*mišpāṭ*],
> but behold, *bloodshed* [*miśpāḥ*];
> for *righteousness* [*ṣᵉdāqāh*],
> but behold, a *cry* [*ṣᵉʿāqāh*]!

God's hopes are profoundly disappointed because God's best hope is an equitable society. What Israel enacts, says the poet, is murder and the desperate cry of the defenseless.

In Isaiah 5:23 (author's translation), in a series of woes, the imagery is quite direct:

> Woe to those who make righteous the guilty for a bribe,
> who remove the righteousness of the righteous.

The affront is systemically perverted courts in which truth is twisted for a price, in which there is no rule of law, no honoring of truth. Social institutions serve those who are in a position to manage them. The situation reflects people who have not come to terms with sovereignty outside their own self-interest, with norms beyond vested interest. Their faith perspective lacks a point of reference outside self and self-interest.

Isaiah 1:21–27 provides the most programmatic lawsuit poem. It indexes Jerusalem's failure (vs. 21, author's translation):

> How she has become a whore,
> the faithful city that was full of justice,
> where righteousness lodged.

The adversative poetry is abrupt. The word "harlot" serves as a contrast to the triad of "righteousness, justice, faithfulness." The city has not become what God intended and hoped for. Then the particulars of harlotry are given (vs. 23):

> Every one loves a bribe
>   and runs after gifts.
> They do not defend the fatherless,
>   and the widow's cause does not come to them.

That is, they do not notice hurt or marginality in social relations. After this drastic critique comes the second step, the dismantling. Such a city will surely be destroyed (from vss. 24–26):

> I will vent/I will avenge/
> I will turn/I will smelt/
> I will remove/I will restore.

The community is put on notice about God's coming judgment. Then comes the third act: *afterward* (vss. 26, 27, author's translation).

> You will be called city of righteousness,
>   faithful city,
> . . . redeemed by justice . . . by righteousness.

The poet lays out a whole scenario of critique (vss. 21–23), dismantling (vss. 24–26a), and new beginning (vs. 26b), but the development comes through shatteringly in moves of harsh discontinuity. The strange thing is that this discontinuity becomes the means to speak about hope and what comes after displacement. Indeed, new *development* requires harsh *displacement,* a breaking of old configurations of power and self-serving value.

(4) Thus the critique, even at its harshest point, carries within it hints of a newness. After the end of ideology, there could be a time of true community, a time of justice, righteousness, and faithfulness. After the *smashing of the false gods,* there could be the *rule of the real God.* Along with the hope of 1:26–27, two other passages may be cited, which show hope arising in the midst of the critique. Isaiah 32:15–17 (author's translation):

When the wind [spirit] is poured upon us from on high . . .
then justice will dwell in the wilderness,
    righteousness will abide in the fruitful field.
The effect of righteousness will be peace,
    the result of righteousness, quietness and trust forever.

The tradition understands. Righteousness, the power to give life, will yield *shalom* and quiet security (cf. 30:15). A newness is possible. The history of hope here is like that of 1:21–27.

(a) Injustice and unrighteousness will lead to dismantling.

(b) Out of the harsh dismantling appear justice and righteousness.

(c) From these comes a new well-being.

The well-being, however, depends on the full end of the destructive arrangement.

Isaiah 33:5–6 is unambiguously positive, which draws it closer to the later Isaiah tradition. It looks to a time after the destruction by the Assyrians:

The Lord is exalted, for he dwells on high;
    he will fill Zion with justice and righteousness;
and he will be the stability ['*mûnath*] of your times,
    abundance of salvation [y°šû'ōth], wisdom and knowledge;
    the fear of the Lord is his treasure.

In the time to come there will be a new city, a new community, a new faith. Yahweh will not quit until a newness is wrought. It is God's righteousness which will be a gift to the city. This righteousness concerns neighborly well-being, which is both free gift and required practice.

(5) This tilt toward newness takes one particular form in First Isaiah that is familiar to us, namely, the king who will come and practice righteousness. This is evident in two well-known texts which are usually not stressed for their note of righteousness:

Of the increase of his government and of peace
    there will be no end,
upon the throne of David, and over his kingdom,
    to establish it, and to uphold it

> with justice and with righteousness
> from this time forth and for evermore. (9:7)

Concerning the shoot from the stump of Jesse, the poet asserts:

> Righteousness shall be the girdle of his waist,
> and faithfulness the girdle of his loins. (11:5)

And yet a third text which is less well known:

> Behold, a king will reign in righteousness,
> and princes will rule in justice. (32:1)

There is no doubt that this is a hopeful promise, but in First Isaiah even this promissory glimpse performs a critical function. It serves to destabilize the present arrangement. The glowing picture of the future, and especially the future king (modeled after Ps. 72), serves to expose the unrighteousness of the present order and the failure of the present rulers. Thus the future promises services to work against, undermine, and subvert the present, to delegitimate its claims, and to dismiss its creditability. In all these ways First Isaiah presents righteousness as a way to speak about unrighteousness in Israel, about Israel's failure to be who it is called to be, and about the power of ideology which seduces, deceives, and prevents a truthful discernment of reality.

IV

Second Isaiah articulates the embrace of pain and finds a new vocation for Israel in it. Our term *righteousness* is used to establish the honest situation of weakness, hurt, vulnerability, failure, and displacement known by the exilic community. The Exile is a setting for faith development because it requires relinquishment and abandonment of self in order that the inscrutable power of God may work a genuine newness.

Second Isaiah's uses of our word are intensely theocentric. They bear witness to the decisive, sovereign way in which God is about to do a thing that will be new and will finally set things as they should be. In moving from First Isaiah to Second Isaiah what strikes one is that the initiative has shifted. Whereas First Isaiah exposes *the false righteousness of Israel,* now Second Isaiah asserts *the sovereign righteousness of Yahweh.* The implication of this shift is that Israel is denied any claim of its own. The poetry diminishes Israel and shows that Israel's righteousness is of little interest to the poet. Such a shift of emphasis marks an important, transformative moment in this poetic portrayal of Israel's situation with Yahweh. On the one hand, the shift reflects the loss of initiative. On the other hand, it portrays a ground for life that lies outside the community so that the faith issue is to accept the gift of righteousness which displaces and nullifies the failed righteousness of Jerusalem.[17]

(1) God is asserted as the utterly righteous one, i.e., the one who has *power for life.* Positive and negative implications come together. Power for life *is indeed available.* Power for life *is not possessed* by Israel, as had been assumed in the older royal attitude.

> The LORD was pleased, for his righteousness' sake
> to magnify his law [torah] and make it glorious. (42:21)

The torah is understood as a source of life, and it is grounded in Yahweh's righteousness (cf. Ps. 19:7).

> And there is no other god besides me,
> a righteous God and a Savior [*môšîa'*],
> there is none besides me. (45:21)

> "Only in the LORD, it shall be said of me,
> are righteousness and strength ['*ōz*]."(45:24)

The righteousness that has basis in Yahweh can save. No other righteousness can save Israel.

(2) The term is used in Second Isaiah, especially in litigation, in lawsuit passages in which Yahweh's righteousness challenges the false claims of righteousness made by others. Thus the usage is polemical. This is in fact an argument about who has the power for life. The argument is made against the nations (41:26; 43:9; 45:19). In these uses, righteousness means to speak what is "right" or "true," but that does not mean factual correctness. It means the authority to say what comes to be. In the third of these texts (45:19) the contrast is with chaos, which obviously has no power for life.[18]

The lawsuit usage also occurs against Israel who continues to

imagine that there is an alternative power for life without facing up
to the righteous will of Yahweh. Against such a claim, the poet has
God say:

> "Put me in remembrance, let us argue together;
>   set forth your case, that you may be proved right."(43:26)

The challenge is issued in sure confidence that Israel has no case to
make and can never be righteous in such a contest:

> [Israel] who swear by the name of the LORD
>   and confess the God of Israel
>   but not in truth ['emeth] or in right. (48:1)

These passages against Israel are uncharacteristic in Second Isaiah,
for the poet most often speaks against false gods and not against
Israel. These two uses (43:26; 48:1), however, suggest a kind of
"mop-up action" on the work of First Isaiah, for the relinquishment
apparently is not yet complete. The old empty, false righteousness
dies hard. This is in contrast to the servant (50:8) who is a model of
faithfulness. God is a sure defense who "vindicates" (ṣaddîq);
therefore none other can make guilty. The servant here is the one
who has accepted the new righteousness of reliance on God.

(3) The abrasive tone of the *juridical language* is more than
offset, however, by the language of assurance in the salvation
oracles. Three examples are offered, each of which invites Israel to
live a life without fear:

> fear not, for I am with you,
>   be not dismayed, for I am your God;
> I will strengthen you, I will help you,
>   I will uphold you with my victorious [ṣedeq] right hand. (41:10)

> > "Listen, you who knew righteousness . . .
> > fear not the reproach of men,
> > and be not dismayed." (51:7, author's translation)

It is adherence to torah which is the source of righteousness, but
even adherence to torah is recognition that righteousness is from
God alone.

> > "In righteousness you shall be established;
> > you shall be far from oppression, for you shall not fear;
> > and from terror, for it shall not come near you." (54:14)

In all three uses it is the righteousness of God which makes Israel's life free from fear. This is quite in contrast to the false righteousness of Israel in First Isaiah, which generated only fear.

(4) Beyond these three motifs—the assertion of *God's sovereignty,* the *dismissal of false righteousness,* and the assertion of God's righteousness which *displaces fear*—Second Isaiah announces the new age, new responsibility, new community, new personhood, when power for life is given by Yahweh and received by Israel. The newness is not fully in hand in Second Isaiah, for Second Isaiah is anticipatory, but it is a certitude to come soon.

(a) The RSV often renders the term *ṣᵉdāqāh* as "deliverance." In 51:1–8 the term is used four times and dominates the poem:

"Hearken to me, you who pursue *deliverance*" (vs. 1)

"My *deliverance* draws near speedily,
my salvation [*yšʿ*] has gone forth,
and my arms will rule the peoples" (vs. 5)

"but my salvation [*yšʿ*] will be for ever
and my *deliverance* will never be ended" (vs. 6)

"but my *deliverance* will be for ever,
and my salvation [*yšʿ*] to all generations" (vs. 8)

(Cf. 46:13, where the parallel with *yšʿ* also occurs.)

These uses make clear that new righteousness is deliverance, rescue, liberation. Yahweh can claim to be sovereign because Yahweh has the power for life. The contrast with First Isaiah is now evident. As only the *righteousness of God can save* in Second Isaiah, so *the righteousness of Israel in First Isaiah can only lead to death.* Faith transformation on the way from First to Second Isaiah is a facing of that truth about righteousness which saves and righteousness which leads to death. This power to liberate is not welcome unless there is an adequate critique of ideology such that it becomes evident that one is not free. Thus First Isaiah aims to create an awareness which lets the news of Second Isaiah have some credibility because it is heard in vulnerability. For the dominant ideology in our culture, autonomy and self-sufficiency are expressed both in military-economic terms and in easy psychologies.

Such a notion of faith and a stagnation of faith transformation not only lead to inaccurate self-regard (cf. Rom. 12:3) but also make community an impossibility.

(b) In other uses the RSV renders our term ṣᵉdāqāh as "victory," which also bespeaks liberation but articulates it more forcefully in terms of a discontinuity. The righteousness of Yahweh is understood as the sending of Cyrus the Persian to permit a homecoming out of Babylon:

> Who stirred up one from the east,
>   whom *victory* [ṣᵉdāqāh] meets at every step? (41:2)

> "In the LORD all the offspring of Israel
>   shall *triumph* [ṣᵉdāqāh] and glory [hll]." (45:25)

> "This is the heritage of the servants of the LORD
>   and their *vindication* [ṣᵉdāqāh] from me, says the LORD." (54:17)

The victory wrought by Cyrus and the derivative homecoming is in contrast to the outcome of Israel's own sad righteousness which is defeat and exile.

(c) Finally we may see that the future promise of deliverance, liberation, victory, and vindication (all images of transformation) is also characterized in other images of the future, each used somewhat ad hoc. Righteousness and salvation are to be given from the heavens like showers, which seems to speak about renewed creation; so the action of Yahweh is not only personal and historical but also cosmic.[19] The whole creation is empowered to life (cf. 45:8). If there were obedience, there would be righteousness like the waves of the sea, i.e., relentless and irresistible, and peace *(shalom)* like a river. Here the power of life is expressed as *shalom* (cf. 48:18). "In righteousness you will be established; you shall be free from oppression and terror" (54:14, author's translation). The social, political dimension is of course foremost. Faith transformation in the Old Testament concerns liberation from oppression. The power of life is incompatible with versions of life that inhibit, restrict, and exploit, which is how it was with those who heard Second Isaiah.

Isaiah 53:11 is a well-known passage concerning the suffering servant. The poem makes a daring rhetorical and theological move. It speaks of the servant, a model of transformed personhood:

he shall see the fruit of the travail of his soul and be satisfied;
by his knowledge shall the *righteous* one, my servant,
make many to be accounted *righteous;*
and he shall bear their iniquities.

The text is difficult, but if we may take the above rendering of it, it is remarkable. The poet has labored mightily to assert that *only God* has the power of righteousness, power for life. It is denied all others. Now in two bold moves the poet asserts that God shares that *power with human persons:* on the one hand, *Cyrus* (41:2) who has the power to liberate; and, on the other hand, *the servant* (53:11) who has the power to make many others righteous. We are not told why, given this jealous claim for Yahweh, these two are so designated, except they had utterly submitted. The servant has power for life because he has been willing to be "deformed," destabilized, and judged by the nations as despised (53:3). *Deformation* is the cost of the power for life. That is another way to say we gain life through its faithful loss (Mark 8:35). Second Isaiah is important for the theme of faith transformation because it articulates the power for life *given from beyond* which opens the future, the power for life *given in vulnerability* and nowhere else.

V

Third Isaiah is a practice of new social imagination. Isaiah 56—66 is a different and difficult literature. Childs and Clements make nothing of it apart from Second Isaiah. I follow Hanson and Achtemeier in seeing it as a poetic, imaginative proposal for a community of the marginal who are able to envision a different shape for life. They have been in exile. Even when they return from exile, they are marginalized by others who also had been in exile, but they are filled with liberated hope and they act with enormous social imagination. The poetry shows a community whose dreams rush out beyond present reality, not unlike the bold political act of Martin Luther King, Jr., who did indeed create a new political reality by his vision, "I have a dream." In terms of faith transformation, the voice speaking in this literature is the voice of persons with faith transformed for passionate social imagination, who have the courage and the freedom to practice life differently.

They know that the way it is is not the way it needs to be. They can begin to dream and shape and image how the world might be.

(1) Righteousness is used negatively to acknowledge that life, as ordered by the dominant priestly group, is unrighteous:

> I will tell of your righteousness and your doings,
>   but they will not help you. (57:12)[20]

The use is ironic. What the priesthood calls righteousness is here exposed as idolatry, the assigning of power to fetishes.

> "Yet they seek me daily,
>   and delight to know my ways,
> as if they were a nation that did righteousness
>   and did not forsake the ordinance of their God." (58:2)

Again the word is used negatively. This righteousness is only "as if." The postexilic community is like a righteous nation, but in fact it is deeply self-indulgent. It is not a delight to God, but only to the community.

> Justice is turned back,
>   and righteousness stands afar off;
> for truth has fallen in the public squares,
>   and uprightedness cannot enter.
> Truth is lacking,
>   and he who departs from evil makes himself a prey.
>   (59:14–15, cf. vs. 9)

These uses of the word attack the dominant party. The attack sounds like First Isaiah. The difference is that there is now an alternative party which is able to practice a different form of faith. Transformed faith results in a countercommunity of those not obedient to the dominant ideology.

(2) The sorry situation need not remain so. This literature insists on a practice of justice and celebrates the power for life that the community can now undertake. It is important that this body of literature begins with a positive appeal, confident of what is possible:

> "Keep justice, and do *righteousness*,
> for soon my salvation [$y\check{s}$] will come,
>   and my *deliverance* [$\check{s}^e d\bar{a}q\bar{a}h$] be revealed." (56:1)

The word *sdq* is used twice. There is an appeal to *do righteousness*.

The ground for so doing is that *God's righteousness* will come soon. Human righteousness is parallel to *justice,* God's righteousness is parallel to *liberation.* Thus the community of the transformed is to practice the power for life.

Then this text becomes quite specific. The new power for life is to open up the temple—the place of life and goods—to all the excluded ones, the foreigners and eunuchs, who have been marginalized (56:3–8). It is an extraordinary invitation. It is an assault on all the old rules of purity (cf. Luke 7:33–35).[21] The text calls for the radical transformation of life and the articulation of new rules and procedures. It suggests that the real transformation of faith is to participate in the new community which overcomes the old unjust order of exclusiveness.

In 60:17–21 this general theme is continued. Our term is used in parallel to *shalom* in verse 17, and in verse 21 it is announced that the righteous who have been excluded shall own the land:

> Your people shall all be righteous;
> they shall possess the land for ever. (60:21)

The new society means the redistribution of land.[22] Indeed, the poetry foresees an inversion of the old community (vss. 17–18, author's arrangement and translation; vs. 22, RSV):

> instead of bronze, gold,
> instead of iron, silver,
> instead of wood, bronze,
> instead of stone, iron,
> instead of violence, peace.
>
> The least one shall become a clan,
> and the smallest one a mighty nation.

Transformed righteousness has to do with the *inversion of society.* The poem anticipates Jesus' assertion that "the last become first." This poetic tradition which reaches into the New Testament stays close to Israel's governing metaphor of land,[23] asserting that the landless ones, the ones who have suffered and found hope in their suffering, will now live in the land.

This kind of freedom for change and newness comes precisely from those who have been exiled, emptied, and made vulnerable, as is evident in Second Isaiah. It is when the liberating righteousness of God is received that this community now has the freedom and power to be open and receptive to God's new thing.

In Isaiah 61:10–11, at the end of the passage that begins with the familiar, "The Spirit of the Lord GOD is upon me," is a lyric celebration of being (author's translation):

> clothed with garments of salvation [*yš˓*],
> covered with the robe of *righteousness*,
> . . . like a bridegroom,
> . . . like a bride,
> so *righteousness* and praise spring up.[24]

This new envisioned society is most graphically enunciated in 65:17–25, which concerns a new heaven, a new earth, a rejoicing Jerusalem (vss. 17–19), new economics (vss. 21–22), and new piety (vs. 24).[25]

Perhaps the most telling metaphor for our study is in 61:3. The verse concerns the inversion of praise instead of grief, gladness instead of mourning, and then, finally, they shall be called *oaks of righteousness*. This is an image of durability, strength, power, and authority. The dream of this literature is to know of people who have the power of life so easily and obviously entrusted to them that every possibility of injustice is unthinkable.[26]

VI

I will conclude with seven reflective comments that derive from the use of the motif of righteousness in the tradition of Isaiah, as that use illuminates matters of faith formation, development, and transformation.

(1) The book of Isaiah provides a grid covering faith transformation. While the subject of this text is regularly Israel, it would seem easily transferable to individual persons. Each person moves through and in some way reenacts the history of this people. That is why we propose this literature as paradigmatic.

(2) *ṣᵉdāqāh, ṣaddîq,* is an appropriate focus for faith development, if understood as power for life. Maturation in faith concerns a more adequate embrace and practice of righteousness. From this

perspective the question becomes, "How and in what ways does the transformation of faith cause people to receive and have the power for life?" *Power for life* is the biblical claim in all transformation and development of faith. This permits us, if we wish, to let the issue of power for life run toward New Testament images of baptism, justification, and resurrection.

(3) The threefold pattern of First-Second-Third Isaiah shows faith transformation in two moves: first, from ideological control to exilic vulnerability; and, second, from exilic vulnerability to restored social imagination.

(4) My concern is to claim that faith formation and development cannot be an empty formal consideration, but are in fact and inevitably must be concrete, substantive issues. Faith formation means something specific with reference to a specific faith formulation. Faith development must be related to this particular God who evokes a particular response of trust and obedience.

The processive moves we have traced in the text make some implicit substantive claims. Faith transformation is not self-contained individualism. It has reference to a sovereign purpose outside of self, which gives gifts and exposes ideology. There is an inscrutable active mystery beyond us that matters decisively for faith maturation. This warns us against any presumed autonomy, which is a ready temptation in our cultural context.

Faith transformation cannot be privatized but always concerns community. This is so for two reasons: first, because the ideology in which one is enmeshed is always a social construction; and, second, because the power for life always means life for others, so that the person is always agent and never simply recipient. We live in a world defined by others. We have gifts which insist upon being shared (cf. 1 Cor. 4:7). This note of faith transformation warns us against any narcissism which believes "I am and there is no other" (cf. Isa. 47:8, 10).

(5) Mature personhood does not come by pilgrimages of continuity, but by abrasion, disruption, and discontinuity which shatter our grasp of things and make us, at key points, not the initiators but the recipients of gifts and surprises that we often do not want to receive.

(6) Our argument is easily related to Romans 10:1–4, where Paul contrasts the righteousness of the law and the righteousness of faith. One may put it thusly: First Isaiah critiques the righteousness of the law, for "law" is always legitimated social interest; Second Isaiah is about the vulnerability of the righteousness of faith; and Third Isaiah is about the practice of righteousness that is not conformed to ideology and law but is transformed so that there need be no more vengeance (Rom. 12:2, 19–21).

(7) The issue that emerges from our study of Isaiah concerns what is the power for life, from whence does it come, and what must be done with it. Our argument is that power for life is given in seasons of vulnerability. New righteousness emerges in exile. It seems a strange way for an oak to grow—but only God can make such a tree. This grid of faith transformation moves by way of dismantling and exile from an oak whose leaf withers (1:30) to sturdy oaks of righteousness (61:3).

3

Blessed Are the History-makers

The historical process is mostly hidden and inscrutable. Enlightenment modes of understanding have led us to imagine that if we could investigate enough we would finally understand how the historical process works. The failure of the Enlightenment has forced us to ask in new ways how history is made. Candidates for history-makers are obvious and well known to us. The oldest candidate as the maker of history is God, and those of us who affirm something of God's sovereignty and providential rule hold to this in some form, even in the face of Enlightenment consciousness. But that is not the whole story. Other candidates for history-makers are expressed in nontheistic, secularized versions of God, whether we speak of the idea of progress, the "classless society," or "the Iron Law of the marketplace." Other candidates (out of the tradition of Carlyle) focus on great personalities, and even Scripture scholars delight to say that David is the first human history-maker. If one focuses on issues of freedom and justice and peace, the question of who makes history is an important and unresolved issue.

I

My interest in the question is both personal and professional. My personal interest was aroused about eight years ago when, as a good parent, I went to a PTA meeting. It was a special night of student performance. The central piece of exhibition was choric reading led by my son's favorite teacher. The reading consisted in various children, one at a time, giving one-liners about American history. They said such things as:

George Washington is the father of our country.
Thomas Jefferson wrote the Declaration of Independence.
Abraham Lincoln freed the slaves and saved the Union.

After each such vignette, the entire fifth grade said in unison, "And America goes on forever." I thought at that moment, and continue to think, "What an odd notion of history and history-makers is being taught in the public schools in Webster Groves." First, I noticed that without exception the history-makers who were named in the one-liners were white, male American officeholders. My son was being taught official history of a highly selective kind.

Second, the refrain, "And America goes on forever," meant that my son was being instructed in ideological history, presuming the absoluteness of a historical institution and a political idea. The two statements—history is made by white male officeholders, and the key conclusion of these one-liners is American durability—together make a very reassuring notion of the historical process. The statements are not disinterested. They are an enormous cover-up in terms of what is left out and of the interests served by such a presentation of history.

Since that moment of awareness, I have had two other thoughts that persist. First, my son's history lesson drove me back to study my own public school history. I can remember what I was taught. I remember the charts I made in order to get it right. History, as I learned it, consisted in the names of all of the American presidents, their parties, their states, and their religion, plus a list of the wars we had won and the territories we had acquired. I studied American history before the Vietnam War. That is, when we could still assert that we had won all our wars. After all, wars are for winning and territories are for taking. It took me a long time in my adult life to begin to see that the sequence of the presidents is not equivalent to history-makers. The list does include some history-makers, but it is difficult to argue that Millard Fillmore or James Buchanan (to name some at a safe distance, though some closer ones might be suggested) made any history that mattered. It was, thus, an important lesson for me to distinguish the official recital which must be learned from the actual history-makers. At many important points in our past the two scarcely overlap at all. In like manner, the mapping of different colors of territory gained (the Louisiana Purchase was always pink on our maps) gives little attention to the imperialism, the blood and oppression, that always goes with the gaining of territory. But I was not taught any of that. Indeed, my teacher did not know that either, because she also was schooled in the uncritical ideology that "America goes on forever."

The other reflective follow-up on the experience of the PTA meeting is more recent. It concerns the explosion of the oral history, tribal history, and folk history of all those groups who have no "recorded glory," which means they did not print the textbooks.[1] There are alternative histories of people who have *suffered* but who never held office and so never made the lists to be recited. We see this with particular reference to Blacks (thanks largely to the impetus of Alex Haley) and to women. There is a massive, variegated form of the history of suffering about which I was taught nothing. Indeed, my history classes and history books proceeded in complete ignorance of this history. About this I have three abiding amazements. First, I am amazed that there really were such histories, as people battled in bold and tough ways to break up power monopolies. That it even happened is remarkable. Second, I am amazed that these histories have been so fully silenced and excluded for such a long time from public awareness. Third, I am amazed that, even with all the intentional and accidental censorship, these historical memories have survived with enormous power and credibility and now function as a critique, a corrective and even an alternative to our ideological history which keeps everything controlled. I have become aware that there is so much to the historical process which I have been denied by the dominant notions of history-making.

All three of these factors—the PTA meeting, my reflection on my education, and the surfacing of histories of hurt—make the question fresh and urgent: who are the history-makers? To what extent is the official tale really a make-believe story designed positively to protect the monopoly and negatively to make the pain less visible and less dangerous? Where the pain is visible, it becomes dangerous. I suspect that where the pain becomes visible, we are close to the history-making process.

II

This set of personal reflections is matched by a professional interest. I am a part of that generation under the influence of Gerhard von Rad[2] and George Ernest Wright,[3] who taught that "God acts in history." As James Barr,[4] Brevard Childs,[5] and many others have shown in retrospect, there are many serious problems with that notion, but the problem is not simply with that particular notion of theology. It really relates to the entire mode of historical-critical methods.[6] I have thought, in that connection, "What have I learned and what have I taught as a scholar about the history-making process in ancient Israel?"

I want to take the period of 626–581 B.C.E. as a test case, with particular reference to Jeremiah. That is the pivotal period in the Old Testament, for in 587 B.C.E. Jerusalem was destroyed and "public history" in Judah came to an abrupt and disastrous end. For my purposes, as will be clear, it is also important that those dates are likely the dates for the prophet Jeremiah.[7] I pose the question concretely: how do we understand and teach the history-making process in this period of Israel's life that climaxed in the loss of temple and king?

I have discovered that what students learn about Judean history in this period consists in two things. Whether one follows Noth, Bright, Herrmann, Anderson, or any other,[8] the first thing is to learn *the time-line.* The time-line is presented in all books on the subject, but our basic source is Second Kings, which in an odd way is a chronological presentation of the kings of Judah and Israel. For our period, one must learn five names in order to have a sense of the shape of history: *Josiah,* the great king who instituted an important reform and died an embarrassing death; his son, *Jehoahaz,* who lasted only three months and was deposed by the Egyptians; Josiah's second son, *Jehoiachim,* who lasted eleven years and who, though he has been judged evil in the Bible, died a peaceful death; his son and Josiah's grandson, *Jehoiachin,* who lasted on the throne only three months and entered a long exile in Babylon; and Josiah's third son, *Zedekiah,* who reigned eleven years and was brutally taken away to Babylon. Now these five kings are useful names to know, along with the dates, in order to get a sense of the order of the period. Judean kings are nice to study, like the monarchs of England, because they all reigned in sequence, one at a time, and can be placed, therefore, on a single time-line. It would hardly be correct, however, to regard them uniformly as history-makers. First of all, two of them, Jehoahaz and Jehoiachin, lasted only three months each. Second, with the possible exception of Josiah, they were all weak kings who, at best, responded and reacted to the history-making that went on around them. They had neither the freedom nor the courage, neither the power nor the imagination, to be history-makers. At the most, they presided over empty forms of power, going through the motions of power without capacity to be history-makers.

Moreover, I suspect the Bible knows that the holders of formal power are not automatically history-makers. One has the sense in the narrative of the Second Kings that we are engaged in a historical process concerning Jersualem that is a process of judgment in which the kings are almost spectators and not really participants. Learning the time-line of ancient Judah may help organize things, but it gives no clue about the history-makers. The time-line is a way to contain and organize data. I can just hear at a PTA meeting in suburban

Jerusalem, five years before the destruction of 587, children in the fifth grade reciting, "And Judah goes on forever." The time-line gives closure and summary, but it does not really show us the dynamics. I have thought that the books of Kings, which are our normative presentation, are engaged only in staging the sequencing and in debunking the royal process.[9] It is as though the books themselves know that the real kings are not history-makers and thereby imply that the books should more properly be entitled *"Kings?"*

Another thing students of the Bible learn is the *headlines,* the ebb and flow of great public events. Headlines are at least as important as time-lines. Now by this I refer to the great movements of empires, the rise-and-fall of nations and kingdoms which is, in fact, simply the relative rearrangement of great masses of political, economic, and military power. These are the headlines that would make the newspapers in both Jerusalem and in Nineveh.

In terms of headlines our period of study is both busy and interesting. The generation of Jeremiah had the unusual opportunity to watch in its lifetime the complete rearrangement of imperial power in the Near East. On the one hand, this is the period of total Assyrian collapse. In 663 Assyrian power under Asshurbanipal extends at its peak clear to Egypt and controls the entire Fertile Crescent. Who would have believed that in fifty years (612) the capital city of Nineveh would be terminated and that in 605 the mop-up of Carchemish would signal the end of the empire? Obviously the headline of the end of the empire is a stunning piece of history-making. On the other hand, who could have foreseen the emergence of imperial Babylon and its remarkable policy of expansionism to the Mediterranean Sea? Before 605 (or perhaps 609) Babylon was scarcely visible; yet by 605 Babylon is abruptly established as the dominant power. The change in the empires was and is news. It marks the end of certain policies and causes discontinuity in the management of power. Every such change brings hope that the new configuration of power will act more humanely.

One has the impression from this twofold headline concerning Assyria and Babylon that the Judean kings are utterly irrelevant.

History is being made elsewhere by other actors, to which the Judean kings have no real access. That must be learned when we are overly impressed with officeholders. So we have the sum of the critical understanding of Judean history for this period. Both *time-line* and *headline* are important. I do not treat either of these lightly. The time-line of Judean kings and the headline of imperial power matter greatly. They must be known in order to understand anything and they no doubt are shaping influences. I suspect that it is the kings in the time-line and the empires in the headline that organize and write the "PTA version" of history.

III

The Old Testament presents to us a very different characterization of history-making. Of course, it would be easy enough to say that it is Yahweh who is the decisive history-maker, and there is truth in that. Certainly the Old Testament centers on the conviction that Yahweh is the decisive history-maker, but Yahweh is not a history-maker in a "supernaturalist" sense. Yahweh's way of history-making is through the processes and agency of human interaction. More specifically, the history-making process in ancient Israel is done through *the voice of marginality* which is carried by prophetic figures and those with whom they make common cause.[10] Two preliminary observations are in order. First, if we take the books of Kings as a clue for the history-making process as presented in ancient Israel, one is struck by two things.

(1) The name of this part of the canon may popularly be called "history," but in Jewish reckoning these are "former prophets." They are the books of prophetic voice. That is what gives shape and drive to historical action in Israel.

(2) The substance of the books of Kings is interesting. While the time-line scheme of the books concerns kings, one has the impression that this literature is not overly impressed with or seriously interested in the kings. The literature is willing to linger and violate the dating scheme by pausing with a prophet. This is evident with Isaiah (2 Kings 18—20), but more stunningly so with

Elijah, Elisha, and Micaiah, whose narratives occupy fully one-third of the corpus.

However, the second observation and the main one I want to make is that the period under study, the period of the five kings, according to the Bible, is dominated by the figure of Jeremiah. No doubt others could present this period without reference to Jeremiah, but not the Bible. My thesis, thus, is that *Jeremiah as a voice of marginality is a history-maker in the sense that the kings could not be,* though he stands outside the time-line and outside every headline.

The real dynamic of the historical process (which lies outside most historical-critical study and which lies outside Yahwistic supernaturalism) is this voice that keeps audible and powerful the hidden, personal, dangerous, subversive sounds that permit the historical process to operate. The official history expressed in the PTA meeting is a contrived history that is in fact ideology and wants to keep things *closed.* The real historical process, however, has as its function to *disclose,* to open, to reveal, to permit the exercise of free choice and the practice of new possibility—precisely the things excluded in the ideological account of time-line and headline. I make the bold proposal, therefore, that Jeremiah does not describe, participate in, or respond to history, but he *makes* history. In what does history consist in this view? In a rather heavy-handed way this is what is meant when we say that prophetic word gets actualized as a deed.[11] This assertion is not magic or supernaturalism but the recognition that when the human, public process is open, new possibilities are brought to light. History-makers thus have as a primary task the penetration of the official ideology that denies and covers over.

(1) What is *disclosed* by the prophetic history-maker always partakes of poetic playfulness and imaginative inventiveness. It violates in substance as well as in form the conventional and administrative categories by which the lid of the status quo is kept on historical vitality. The truth of this historical process is always much more raw, ragged, and ambiguous than official summaries and reports can acknowledge.

(2) This disclosed material of human hurt and suffering, human hope and amazement, is the stuff of history. One does not have genuine history in any human sense unless there is free play of such human ingredients, for those are the ingredients which make newness possible in the human community. It is clear, then, that the kings who are voices of certitude and who work to banish or deny the ambiguity are in fact not history-makers, but are history-preventers.

(3) In every generation, our own included, the people who make the time-line, the people who sponsor and benefit from the headline, want to manage the process, deny the hurt, eradicate the ambiguity. In a word, they badly want to nullify and silence the voice from outside which keeps calling attention to that for which the system cannot account. Thus, the conflict between king and prophet is not simply a conflict over ethical substance. It is also and primarily a conflict about processes of interaction, modes of communication, and judgments about what matters in the ordering of public life. The history-makers are those who have the capacity and courage to *disclose* the human processes. The dominant voices, however, are those which want to *close* the human process in the interest of order and the protection of a monopoly which always needs to be guarded. My preliminary judgment is that when the disclosing process is halted, history-making comes to an end. Where history-making ends, society is at the edge of losing its humanness. Thus, history-makers as I characterize them are always set in contexts where the agents of domination want to stop the free play of the historical process.

There are, of course, several ways to silence such voices of disclosure which keep history open. The silencing can happen by priestly control, by political intimidation, by theological orthodoxy, by economic oppression, and by technical reason. Every established power has a vested interest in stopping the historical process. The wonder is that in ancient Israel (and often since) the voices of disclosure are not silenced. The result is that imperial power is always in jeopardy. Somewhere, in a notice I cannot now locate, Karl Popper has said a remarkable thing about history-making—

namely, that all history is written by the winners, the people on top, with one exception. That exception, says Popper, is the history of Jesus and his community. I would extend Popper's observation to say it is the history of Yahweh and the community of Yahweh that writes history from underneath (cf. Ps. 82).

The makers of history in this understanding include *Yahweh* who is the God allied with the poor (cf. Jer. 2:34; 5:28; 22:16), *Jeremiah* the prophet who is allied with that underneath perception of historical reality, and the *outsiders* who perceive the world differently.[12] Notice that in such an understanding the people on the time-line and in the headline are not history-makers. If anything, they are the ones who want to stop the historical process, reduce the freedom of the historical process by reducing everything to a closed, fixed ideology. The very ones whom we may expect to make history are the ones who do not want history to happen, who fear history, because the historical process jeopardizes our control and calls into question present configurations of power and present arrangements of monopoly.

IV

Jeremiah and those linked to him are the history-makers. A study of the Jeremiah tradition suggests five factors that belong to the history-making process.

(1) Jeremiah experiences and articulates a profound sense of *anguish, pathos, and incongruity that touches him quite personally.* Recent scholarship may be correct in saying that we know very little about the personality of Jeremiah.[13] It cannot be doubted, however, that this text is the peculiar voice of someone who lived close to, noticed, and took seriously the reality of life around him. The text of Jeremiah is no nameless oracle from God. It is the disclosure of God mediated through a self-knowing, self-caring agent. Such an agent has not succumbed to the dominant definitions of reality, to the conventional epistemology, or to the policies and values which tend to deny and cover up. This voice is from one who has noticed the odd, marginal realities that are not contained in or are nullified by the comprehensive claims of the regime. Said another way, this voice has kept enough distance from dominant definitions to be

able to say with a different voice precisely the things which are mostly denied. It is no wonder that such a history-maker as Jeremiah does and says things that are unsettling, even unacceptable, because such history-makers tend to destabilize by insisting on reality that has otherwise been declared to be unreality.

In the brief cry of woe in 15:10–12, Jeremiah has a sense about himself that he is forever an outsider in conflict, a stranger to dominant values: "Woe is me, my mother, that you bore me, a man of strife and contention to the whole land! I have not lent, nor have I borrowed, yet all of them curse me" (vs. 10). This is a cry of anguish about the shape and destiny of history-making. Why am I always in question, under assault, at risk? No answer is offered, but the allusion to "iron and bronze" in verse 12 at least hints that the reason is related to his calling, for in 1:18 it is he who is made to be iron and bronze for his vocation.

In 12:1, Jeremiah raises a famous question which lingers among us:

> Why does the way of the wicked prosper?
> Why do all who are treacherous thrive?

This is the most explicit articulation of the theodicy question in Israel prior to Job.[14] To raise the question of theodicy, the issue of God's justice, is to raise the issue about the essential arrangement of social power in the world. That is both theologically and sociologically a subversive question because it suggests that the system is not working in an acceptable way. In the case of Jeremiah it is especially noteworthy that the issue is not raised as a theoretical or speculative notion, as it is often portrayed. It is raised, rather, in relation to one's sense of being assaulted, abused, and treated unfairly (cf. 11:18–23). The general question grows out of a personal concern which is powerfully brought to speech.

This sense of personal anguish about the context in which Jeremiah lives is evident in the poem of 4:19–22. Jeremiah takes his listeners inside his own troubled awareness:

> My anguish, my anguish! I writhe in pain!
> Oh, the walls of my heart!

> My heart is beating wildly;
>   I cannot keep silent;
> for I hear the sound of the trumpet,
>   the alarm of war.
> Disaster follows hard on disaster,
>   the whole land is laid waste.
> Suddenly my tents are destroyed,
>   my curtains in a moment.
> How long must I see the standard,
>   and hear the sound of the trumpet?
> "For my people are foolish,
>   they know me not;
> they are stupid children,
>   they have no understanding.
> They are skilled in doing evil,
>   but how to do good they know not."

The internal sense of a trembling body gripped in terror is linked to the external reality of an invading army. The poetry is not a trivial sharing of one's internal life, but a means to make a statement about the reality of public life for those who are able to notice. Jeremiah's twisting stomach is a source from which to announce that things are not well. The enemy is near, even if the powerful ones cannot notice. It makes the poet sick.

Finally, in addition to Jeremiah's cry of woe, his lingering question of theodicy, and his personal anguish, we may observe the abrasiveness and poignancy of Jeremiah's prayers, which are complaints addressed to God.[15] As Jeremiah is restive about what is happening on earth, so he is restless in the face of heaven. As he refuses to accept the conventions of the human community, so he refuses to accept the conventional ways of God. He accuses God of not being equitable. He prays for vengeance upon the wrongdoers because he knows he is entitled to better than what he has received. In 20:14–18 Jeremiah pushes his sense of his historical location to the edge of what is acceptable by cursing his birth and wishing for his death. On all these counts Jeremiah is so much in touch with his own pain and the pain of his community that he dares to think the unthinkable, to utter the unutterable. That is a mark of a history-maker.

(2) Like every history-maker Jeremiah has confidence in the

moral coherence of the world. He believes passionately that there is a fiber of justice and righteousness that persists in the historical process and in public life, which finally cannot be violated, mocked, or nullified. It does seem in his time (as it often does) as though the world is ordered in other ways, as though the historical process is without moral significance, as though public life can be administered by might, technique, knowledge, control, intimidation, self-interest, brutality, pragmatism. It does seem so. Jeremiah did not have to look far to see that.

This, however, is not the way of history-makers. Such a way leads only to cynicism, resignation, and inhumanity. History-makers are of another kind. Jeremiah argues against such cynicism. On occasion he appeals for change:

> "If you remove your abominations from my presence,
>   and do not waver,
> and if you swear, 'As the LORD lives,'
>   in truth, in justice, and in uprightness,
> then nations shall bless themselves in him,
>   and in him shall they glory." (4:1–2)

> "For if you truly amend your ways and your doings, if you truly execute justice one with another, if you do not oppress the alien, the fatherless or the widow, or shed innocent blood in this place, and if you do not go after other gods to your own hurt, then I will let you dwell in this place, in the land that I gave of old to your fathers for ever." (7:5–7)

Both of these passages appeal for change. Both of them are presented in an "if-then" structure, indicating that human conduct matters decisively for the outcome of public life.

Most often, however, Jeremiah recommends no change. He simply exposes, condemns, and indicts. He is sure this community has chosen death:

> "How can I pardon you?
>   Your children have forsaken me,
>   and have sworn by those who are no gods.
> When I fed them to the full,
>   they committed adultery
>   and trooped to the houses of harlots.

> They were well-fed lusty stallions,
>> each neighing for his neighbor's wife.
>
> Shall I not punish them for these things?
>> says the LORD." (5:7–9)

Likely the poet here uses the imagery of harlotry both concretely and as a metaphor for self-sufficiency.

The condemnation falls heavily on unprincipled leadership which uses public office to bestow privilege on those who control the public monopoly:

> "Every one is greedy for unjust gain,
> and from prophet to priest,
>> every one deals falsely.
>
> They have healed the wound of my people lightly,
>> saying, 'peace, peace,'
>> when there is no peace." (6:13–14)

The public leadership is engaged in policies which are a massive cover-up of social and moral reality. All of it is cosmetics. Then Jeremiah adds this poignant indictment:

> "Were they ashamed when they committed abomination?
>> No, they were not at all ashamed;
>> they did not know how to blush.
>
> Therefore they shall fall among those who fall." (6:15)

When a society loses its capacity to blush, it indicates that all norms outside of self-interest have collapsed. Or again,

> They bend their tongue like a bow;
>> falsehood and not truth has grown strong in the land;
>
> for they proceed from evil to evil,
>> and they do not know me, says the LORD. (9:3)

The history-makers have always been those who could speak covenantal truth to power. The principalities and powers always manage to consolidate enough power, enough hardware, and enough ideology to imagine themselves immune to the battering, raging, and insistence of moral power. History-makers raise inescapable questions about the shapes of power and well-being in history. Did anyone imagine that power could save ancient

Jerusalem when the rottenness was so apparent? Does anyone imagine there are enough tanks in Poland finally to crush the dreams for equity? Does anyone imagine there are enough means for repression in South Africa to halt the moral power for justice among disinherited Blacks? Are there those who seriously think that the yearning of peasants for land in Central America will finally be stopped by United States' aid to unprincipled oligarchies? To some that will sound all too reductionist and simplistic, but history-makers are neither subtle nor impressed with moral waffling. They are able to spot precisely the point of moral failure and the corresponding point of moral possibility. Jeremiah is appalled at all the others who are so seduced that they do not see:

> "For my people are foolish,
>   they know me not;
> they are stupid children,
>   they have no understanding.
> They are skilled in doing evil,
>   but how to do good they know not." (4:22)

Where they do not know how to do good, they will be crushed by the moral power relentlessly at work in the historical process.

(3) Jeremiah, like other history-makers, *asserts the raw rule of God* in the historical process. There is a tendency for the rulers of this age to melt the reality of God down into the system of governance, so that the present order comes to be an embodiment of God's will, i.e., the created order. Cushman[16] has traced this temptation in modern subjectivism, from the time of the Reformation until its sharp articulation in Feuerbach, that God is only our best projection.

More immediately, religion in our time tends to be reduced to privatism, personalism, and immanentism, so that God is remarkably congenial to the way things are. We have almost no language left and no space in which to speak about the freedom and abrasiveness of God, the judgment of God, or the notion that God has a will of God's own and a work to do that is not dependent on our efforts and policies (cf. Isa. 55:6–9). The history-makers do not appeal to such an anemic God. They insist that God has a purposeful and tenacious will that is being worked out in public processes. This will of God is free and unfettered and will have its say as it moves in the direction of justice and humaneness.

God's free will is dangerous and threatening. Jeremiah must use dangerous speech and subversive images to shake the theological indifference of those who have domesticated God. To bring God to speech in this way is not, first of all, to argue a policy point. Much more, it is to reopen the field of public imagination so that policy formation is not one-dimensional. The poet speaks this way about the raw sovereignty:

> "A lion has gone up from his thicket,
>   a destroyer of nations has set out;
>   he has gone forth from his place
> to make your land a waste;
>   your cities will be ruins
>   without inhabitant.
> For this gird you with sackcloth,
>   lament and wail;
>   for the fierce anger of the Lord
>   has not turned back from us." (4:7–8)

The "lion" here may indeed be mighty Babylon, but the end of the unit makes clear that the engine for the lion can only be Yahweh. Or consider this poem in which Yahweh is clearly intended as the subject:

> Therefore a lion from the forest shall slay them,
>   a wolf from the desert shall destroy them,
> A leopard is watching against their cities.
>   every one who goes out of them shall be torn in pieces;
> because their trangressions are many,
>   their apostasies are great. (5:6)

The metaphorical power of the poem is enormous. The threat of God's intervention comes all at once as a lion, wolf, and leopard.

Alongside these images of dangerous beasts, Jeremiah makes use of the metaphor of illness, which he variously describes as heart trouble and sickness unto death (cf. 6:7; 8:18–22).[17] The image of God as being sick with the sickness of Judah is a poetic attempt, not to link the reality of God to the dimensions of well-being and power as we are wont to do, but to lodge God precisely at the place society wants to deny and cover up. God functions as a principle of savage honesty in a scheme of cover-up. This God is a God of distance, as well as one close at hand (23:23).[18] This God is one who not only undergirds the present arrangement but also stands removed from it in order to assess and perhaps to assault.

The role of God in prophetic poetry is to function as a norm and agent for "deabsolutizing" the pretensions of the Jerusalem establishment. The tendency of every settled arrangement is to become permanent and absolute, beyond every criticism. Where God is kept rawly sovereign by the poets, however, one can deabsolutize. One becomes aware that, vis-à-vis the dangerous holiness of God, this present arrangement may not claim so much nor be taken so seriously.

The point of the argument is not that all history-makers are believers in our particular articulation of God. Where they are not believers, I submit that the serious history-makers must in each case appeal to something equivalent to this raw, undomesticated sovereignty of God as a principle from which to criticize the present order. This may take quite secular forms and indeed must take secular forms when God has been fully co-opted by those who want to halt history at a certain moment. What the history-makers face is not so much a genuine atheism as it is an idolatry in which the sovereign God is captive to schemes of social control.[19] Against such idolatry one may either assert the dangerous sovereignty of God (as Jeremiah does) or deny the sovereignty of a god so easily co-opted.

(4) Thus far I have claimed that serious history-makers are passionate poets, moral energizers, and dangerous theologians. Now I submit that history-makers also *engage in discerning social analysis.* They may not have all the elitist tools of modern social theory, as we might expect or wish, but they are able to look at social policy and social crisis and read through them to see what in fact is going on. That is, they are peculiarly attentive to the work of social ideology, the self-deception of propaganda, the narcotic effect of religion, and the management of moral persuasion in the interest of social monopoly. These people, whom we call prophets in the Old Testament, are not ignorant rabble-rousers; rather they operate with a sophisticated sense of social reality. Bernard Lang

on Amos,[20] Hans Walter Wolff on Micah,[21] and Robert Coote on Amos[22] have shown the acute analysis of the issues that operate in those prophetic texts. I stress this point because it appears to me that, with our paranoia about Marxian analysis, Americans (and perhaps especially liberals) are incredibly uninformed and therefore naive. By denying ourselves some sense of social analysis, it becomes exceedingly difficult to recognize what is going on among us and to mount an alternative.

Three items from Jeremiah may be subsumed under this point. First, Jeremiah is relentlessly committed to the notion that God has given Judah over into the hands of Babylon (cf. 25:9; 27:6). This need not be read as a supernaturalism. One can also say that Jeremiah had discerned the sure flow of power toward that empire and that he discerned this general shift in world power to be resonant with God's sovereign purpose. This is not supernaturalism, but it also is not mere pragmatism. Jeremiah had concluded early on that resistance to Babylon was futile, precisely because it was in opposition to the will of God. History-makers have some sense of the flow of the historical process in the long haul and are very sure about where history is headed. They are able to see that direction in spite of the ideology which argues otherwise.

Second, in Jeremiah 27—28 the prophet has a rather extraordinary exchange and confrontation with Hananiah, another prophet. This confrontation illustrates a particular point. Hananiah has been judged by the canonical text to be false. That is how the Bible reads the matter. What Hananiah did was simply to assert that exile could not last long or be very serious because God loves Judah. Scholars are wont to say that Hananiah is simply asserting in his situation what Isaiah said earlier. The difference is that when Isaiah spoke the same message a century earlier, it was judged the true word of God. What makes the message of Hananiah false? In retrospect, what makes it false is that Hananiah was propounding a view of history that was not informed by what was in fact happening.[23] Jeremiah is "true" because he truly discerned that the great fact of his time was *an ending,* a serious disruption that would put chosen people into exile, off the land. Social analysis can penetrate old truth that subsequently turns out to be wishful thinking and ideology.

Third, in one of the most radical texts Jeremiah the history-maker poses the question: what is it that is definitional for kingship (22:13–17)? That is in fact a quite sophisticated theoretical question: what are the true marks of legitimate power?[24] He asks the question by appeal to two recent kings, Jehoiachim and his father, Josiah, who stand in total contrast. The rule of Jehoiachim offers this answer: kingship consists in spacious rooms, windows, cedar, vermillion. Kingship consists in economic luxury and the visible accoutrements of office. The issue is joined by the prophet's counterproposal based on Josiah: kingship is marked by justice and righteousness, by attending to the poor and needy. The contrast could not be sharper. The king may preside over prosperity, but that is not an adequate measure of legitimacy.

On all three counts—discernment of the Babylonian flow of power, the reality of an ending of an arrangement so long treasured, and the marks of legitimate power—we see that this poetic passion is under the discipline of and informed by a very serious and discerning social criticism. That kind of discipline is indispensable if the dominant ideology is to be seriously challenged. Passion without the tools of analysis and social criticism is an unreliable way to make history.

(5) Finally, history-makers have a *bold conviction about alternative possibilities which go under the name of hope*. While such history-makers may see clearly that things are deeply wrong, while they may not see how in any way a turn can happen, they are characteristically not voices of despair. History-makers and historical action do not proceed out of despair but out of hope that acts against the data at hand.

It is astonishing that Jeremiah can assert in so many ways that the sure end is coming upon Judah, temple, and kingship and yet can find ways to articulate a future precisely out of the failure.[25] This way of speaking is not simply pastoral consolation offered to exiles, though it is that.[26] It also is not simply social analysis, though that is involved. Rather, it is a sense that the failure of the order is not equivalent to or coterminal with the defeat of God. God's purpose abides in the midst of historical chaos and will finally work through the chaos to create a fresh social possibility (cf. Isa. 45:18–19).[27]

Two such texts in the tradition of Jeremiah may be cited. In 29:4–9 the prophet sends a letter to the exiles. In it he counsels them to settle in and get used to exile. The displacement is real and serious and will last. They are to entertain no wishful thinking about its quick end and a "return to normalcy," as the royal ideologues suggested (among whom is Hananiah). Then in verses 10–14, in some of the most formidable language of the tradition, the oracle announces:

> "I will fulfill to you my promise and bring you back to this place. For I know the plans I have for you, says the LORD, plans for welfare and not for evil, to give you a future and a hope. Then you will call upon me and come and pray to me, and I will hear you. You will seek me and find me; when you seek me with all your heart, I will be found by you, says the LORD, and I will restore your fortunes and gather you from all the nations and all the places where I have driven you, says the LORD, and I will bring you back to the place from which I sent you into exile."

The affirmation of exile is clear. Nothing painful is denied, but in the character and resolve of God, exile is no more the last word than is the old temple arrangement. There will be a new social possibility wrought not by political strategy but by God's free capacity to work beyond visible constructs.[28] It is that freedom of God which gives a future and a hope.

In 24:1–10 we are given what may be an even more daring act of hope. The vision the prophet sees concerns good figs and bad figs. These are taken as ciphers for elements of the Jewish community. What is unexpected is that the Jews left in the land are rejected, whereas the displaced ones in exile are taken as the wave of the future whom God will now plant and build. This assertion of God's fresh resolve, no doubt filtered through the interest of the exilic community, represents a radical move about the future, asserting that the community which seemed to be dead, punished, and devalued (exiled) is the community out of which Yahweh will begin again the historical process of community building.[29] The rejected, displaced ones are the ones out of which God's new age will be constructed.[30] This act of hope, so indispensable for history-makers, is a theological statement about God's resolve. It is at the same time a historical judgment about the materials (exiles) through which God's newness comes.

In sum, I propose that Jeremiah provides a paradigm for history-makers around these five items:

(1) A profound sense of anguish, pathos, and incongruity that touches him personally.
(2) Confidence in the moral coherence of the world.
(3) Assertion of the raw sovereignty of God in the historical process.
(4) Capacity for discerning social analysis and criticism.
(5) Bold conviction about an alternative possibility that goes under the name of hope.

It will be clear that these elements are in fact and are regularly perceived to be subversive. History-making, as I understand it, is a process of subverting public and institutional forms of power that have become frozen and absolutized in favor of some at the expense of others. Jeremiah is subversive as a history-maker (38:4), even as his vivid language points to the transcendent history-maker who moves against every monopoly.

V

History-makers like Jeremiah (a) take the time-line and the headline seriously but not normatively; (b) maintain some critical distance from the dominant definitions in order to have space for alternative thinking and liberated imagination; (c) live at the edge of society where alternatives are thinkable and possible in terms of an imagination not yet co-opted. Their history-making process I characterize in this way: it is the free give-and-take of parties over new sets of power settlements that are made possible through honest, risky communication. That, of course, is not a conventional understanding of history which is preoccupied with lists of officials and celebrations of wars and defense of old spheres. My urging is that, from its basic premises on, the Bible offers us a very different notion of history, that history is the arena of the Holy One allied with the marginal people to create newness. That is why in the Old Testament it is the prophets who speak the history-creating word while kings are mostly left to preside over the shells of power. That is why in the New Testament Jesus is represented as the real history-maker against those who manage the ceremonies (cf. Matt. 23:27) of what used to be. This way of understanding history-makers applies not only to such ancient poets as Jeremiah but also to people whom we may identify in our own cultural context, who make history and can be understood in the categories we have found in Jeremiah.

The kinds of history-makers who are blessed include such dangerous people as:

Rosa Parks, who in Montgomery refused to move to the back of the bus and changed the shape of our lives;

Lech Welesa, for whom there are not enough Polish tanks to stifle the dream of freedom;

Betty Williams, who with Mairead Corrigan has announced in Belfast, "It is enough";

Molly Blackburn, a white South African who lost her life because of her passion for racial justice.

These are outsiders who make history. They are in the company of Jesus and the "people" (as distinct from the "scribes and principal men" in Luke 19:47–48) who daily call them blessed.

If these, then, are the history-makers, who are the others? Who are the ones on the time-line and in the headline—to whom my son in grade school referred with the refrain "America goes on forever"? What are they up to? I submit that the dominant tendency of such voices is to be *history-stoppers*, not *history-makers*.[31] That is, their goal is most often to stop the historical process, to end the give-and-take, to silence the power questions, to terminate the serious conversation, so that things can be frozen at a particular time and place for the benefit of some at the expense of others. The history-stoppers are noticed more often than the history-makers, for they command attention and seem important and powerful. It is an uneven match, but the bet of biblical faith is that the history-makers who seem so helpless will finally overcome the history-stoppers. The history-makers regularly experience crucifixion at the hands of the history-stoppers, but they are judged blessed in the end, greeted in resurrection, for they shall see God.

Next to Disney World in Orlando, Florida, is Epcott, the "City of Tomorrow," a dazzling presentation of technological possibilities of extraordinary kinds. A friend of mine asked one of the management people, "Why, with all this technology, is there nothing in any of your exhibits about the politics of tomorrow? It is completely missing." The response was, "We don't want anything as complicated and messy as politics in our city of tomorrow, because we want it clean and simple." Precisely! The history-makers insist on the political process, messy as it is, as the only way to human newness. The history-stoppers want to invoke technique and call in the wisdom teachers,[32] but where *history* is stopped by *technique* we are all diminished and left in despair.

In his eloquent Harvard commencement address, Carlos Fuentes[33] has made a plea that North Americans honor the history-making process now under way in Central America. He said, "The source of change in Latin America is not in Moscow or Havana; it is history."[34]

> Reality is not the product of an ideological phantasm. It is the result of history. And history is something we have created ourselves. We are thus responsible for our history. No one was present in the past. But there is no living present with a dead past. No one has been present in the future. But there is no living present without the imagination of a better world. We both made the history of this hemisphere. We must both remember it. We must both imagine it. We need your memory and your imagination or ours shall never be complete. You need our memory to redeem your past, and our imagination to complete your future. . . . Let us remember one another. Let us respect one another. Let us walk together outside the night of oppression and hunger and intervention.[35]

History-makers dare to walk outside the night of repression and hunger. History-making looks to the time when "they shall all know me, from the least of them to the greatest, says the LORD; for I will forgive their iniquity, and I will remember their sin no more" (Jer. 31:34). History is the painful process of remembering, forgiving, forgetting, and moving on.[36]

4

Living Toward a Vision: Grief in the Midst of Technique

The Jewish Bible, the Christian Old Testament, is fundamentally a literature of hope, yet, at least in Christian circles the Old Testament has such a caricatured reputation as a tradition of law, judgment, and wrath. I want to explore this tradition of hope, as I judge it to be a very odd phenomenon, a problem in the Western tradition, and a great resource for our present cultural situation.

The dominant intellectual tradition of the West, that of hellenistic philosophy out of which has come the ground of reasonableness for science, is not a tradition of hope. It is a tradition of *order* which seeks to discern, understand, decipher, know, and, if possible, master and control. Thus the biblical tradition lives in considerable tension with the dominant intellectual tradition and often has not had its full say. It is clear that *order* and *hope* are not about the same thing, nor are they easily held together. It is clear that both order and hope are essential for viable human community. We are in a season when the *urge for order* seems nearly to squeeze out the *voice of hope*. For that reason, to reflect on this tradition of hope is an important exercise for us.

Jews (and Christians after them) are a people of hope, but they can be a people of hope only if they are not alienated from and ignorant of their tradition. Therefore it is important to identify the shape and substance of that hope. In what follows I will consider the main texts of hope and then explore three major issues related to them.

I

I begin by distinguishing five elements of hope literature in the Old Testament, not all of equal power or significance. This catalog suggests how pervasive, even definitional, are the hope dimensions of this faith.

(1) Von Rad[1] and Westermann[2] have established that the Genesis narratives about Abraham, Isaac, and Jacob are essentially narratives of hope. The overriding substance of this literature is a promise from God that is open-ended in its scope and definitions and is brought to fulfillment only by the fidelity of God. The substance of the promise is variously an heir, a great name, a new land, a community of blessing among the nations.[3]

Alt[4] has shown that the God disclosed in the Genesis narratives is a God who makes promises and who keeps them. This God is not to be linked in any way with totemism or the primitive religions that the historians of religion and the structuralists consider. Paul Ricoeur[5] has shown that from the very outset this God, unlike so many around, is not an abiding presence but a speaker of a new word who breaks open all that is settled, routine, and conventional. This is a God of *kerygma,* of a message that transforms reality. The most dramatic examples of this powerful promise are related to Abraham. In Genesis 12:1–3[6] Abraham is summoned by this speaker of promise to leave his natural habitat and to go in naked trust to a different place, a place not even yet identified. In 18:1–15[7] it is asserted, by means of a rhetorical question, that nothing is impossible for God. It is promised that this God has the power to make things new by his promise, so new that birth displaces the long-standing and hopeless barrenness of Sarah and Abraham. The stories are not magical or supernatural in any conventional sense. Rather they are recitals of the memory of the inexplicable happenings which have gone on in this family of hope. One can see how such memories enable this community to hope against all data and to believe that the *hopelessness* of the data never rules out a different *possibility*. God can indeed work a newness against all of the data. God can shatter the known world in order to establish a new historical possibility. Jews and Christians cling to such an affirmation.

Israel is portrayed as a people who sometimes doubt and resist this wonder of God, but on the whole Israel in these narratives is ready to receive the word, trust the promise, and act in hope. Indeed, Israel's history in these early tales consists in responding to such impossible words and being willing to depart the known world on the basis of such a summons. That is what we have meant by a recital of "God's mighty deeds." In these tales the central dynamic of biblical faith is established. In the very character of God there is a push and an impetus to violate, overthrow, and depart the established order for the sake of a newness not yet comprehended or in hand.

(2) The prophetic texts of the eighth to sixth century B.C.E., in lyrical promise passages, state the themes of promise, hope, and trust even more baldly.[8] Here they are not encased in old narratives; they are poems that have no intent other than to tell the story of the future. They characteristically begin with "Behold, the days are coming," or "In that day." This rhetorical pattern affirms that there will be a day of turn in which the dominant order of things as we have known it will be terminated. God has no final commitment to the present ordering of things, which will be drastically displaced by a wholly new order. The new order is not at all to be established by human plan, human knowledge, or human power. It is the inscrutable, irresistible work of God. Again, like the Genesis stories, the push and impetus come only from the mystery of God and from nowhere else.

The themes of prophetic hope are fairly constant. There is nothing here that is private, spiritual, romantic, or otherworldly. It is always social, historical, this-worldly, political, economic. The dream of God and the hope of Israel are for the establishment of a new social order which will embody peace, justice, freedom, equity, and well-being. Thus, not only is the tradition formally hope-filled, but also the substance of that hope is clear. In some ways the substance of the hope as *a new social world* is even more radical than the formal claim of promise itself. We may cite only some examples of these prophetic visions.

(a) Perhaps the best known is the vision of peace in Micah 4:1–5, which for the most part is reiterated in Isaiah 2:1–5.[9] Its phrasing is well known:

> they shall beat their swords into plowshares
> and their spears into pruning hooks;
> nation shall not lift up sword against nation,
> neither shall they learn war any more. (vs. 3)

Micah then adds a shrewd economic note from the perspective of the peasant community[10] (which is not in the Isaiah parallel) about the cost of such anticipated disarmament:

> they shall sit every man under his vine and under his fig tree,
> and none shall make them afraid. (vs. 4)

The poet recognizes that serious disarmament requires a lowered standard of living, so that rapacious greed ends, taxes can be reduced, and people are satisfied with a little, just a vine and a fig tree. Yet they are in safety and well-being. The poem is an incredible act of hope. One cannot see how one can get from here to there, either in the ancient world or in our own time, but such hope is precisely a "conviction of things not seen" (Heb. 11:1).

(b) A second, very different promise is found in Isaiah 19:23–25.[11] It is the most sweeping geopolitical assertion in the Old Testament and can be heard in all its radicalness if one listens with an ear to the present situation in the same geographical locus:

> In that day there will be a highway from Egypt to Assyria, and the Assyrian will come into Egypt, and the Egyptian into Assyria, and the Egyptians will worship with the Assyrians.

> In that day Israel will be the third with Egypt and Assyria, a blessing in the midst of the earth, whom the LORD of hosts has blessed, saying, "Blessed be Egypt my people, and Assyria the work of my hands, and Israel my heritage."

In this remarkable vision the poet takes the words properly applied only to beloved Israel, words like "my people" and "work of my hands," and applies them to other nations which are in fact enemies.

The dream is for a time when the barriers of fear, insecurity, and inequality have been overcome, when there is free access among the nations who are traditional enemies. Again the hope of biblical faith is incredible, for one cannot see, among ancient empires or among contemporary nation-states, how this can come about. But Israel at its best, when informed by its memory, lives toward a vision which is as certain as is God's own word (cf. Isa. 55:10–11).

(c) In a very different idiom is the vision of Ezekiel 34:25–31:

> "I will make with them a covenant of peace and banish wild beasts from the land, so that they may dwell securely. . . . And the trees of the field shall yield their fruit, and the earth shall yield its increase, and they shall be secure in their land; and they shall know that I am the LORD, when I break the bars of their yoke, and deliver them from the hand of those who enslave them. . . . And you are my sheep, the sheep of my pasture, and I am your God, says the Lord GOD."

This is a promise of a covenant of *shalom,* of well-being and prosperity. The promise moves in two rather remarkable directions. On the one hand, it has a hope for the restoration of creation, the renewal of the ecological process, so that the field and the earth will bring forth abundantly. On the other hand, this renewal has a political component. The banishment of "wild beasts" may be read literally or as a metaphor for rapacious political power. The breaking of "the yoke" means an end to oppression. The promise thus articulates restoration for both history and nature, for both politics and fertility, in which all relationships will be as they were envisioned in the uncontaminated anticipation of the creation narrative of Genesis 1.

(d) Finally, the promise of Isaiah 65:17–25 is the most sweeping of the prophetic promises I will mention. It begins with these words (vss. 17–18):

> "For behold, I create new heavens
> and a new earth;
> and the former things shall not be remembered
> or come into mind.
> But be glad and rejoice for ever
> in that which I create;
> for behold, I create Jerusalem a rejoicing,
> and her people a joy."

As the promise continues, the new heaven and new earth are characterized by a new economic order in which none will usurp the produce of others, by a new order of health without death in childbirth and with no infant mortality, and by a new understanding with God such that God shall be present and available at every point of need. This poet has dreamed the most undisciplined, liberated vision of them all. The prophets are resolute and unanimous. The way it is, is not the way it will be. It is promised that there will be a decisive change in the shape of human life on earth.

(3) The great prophetic hopes are pushed one step further later in the faith of Israel as prophecy becomes apocalyptic.[12] Apocalyptic is the most extreme form of hope in the Bible, and the most misunderstood. It is misunderstood by those who do not understand that this is poetic imagination and who instead want it to be a hard prediction to be assessed in detail. Such a view misunderstands both the character of the literature and the nature of hope in the Bible. The biblical way of hope is to dream large dreams about the powerful purposes of God, but they are not designs, blueprints, or programs. To make them such is to deny God's free governance over the future.

Apocalyptic literature is not pervasive in the Old Testament, but it flourishes in the period between the testaments.[13] Zechariah 14:8–9 offers a characteristic hope for Israel:

> On that day living waters shall flow out from Jerusalem, half of them to the eastern sea and half of them to the western sea; it shall continue in summer as in winter.
> And the LORD will become king over all the earth; on that day the LORD will be one and his name one.

This imagery is so radical that it is pushed outside the historical process. In this anticipation the waters of life flow like the rivers of life in Genesis 2, but now the source is the holy temple city. The great vision is that Yahweh, the God of Israel, will rule the nations. This hope is not unlike prophetic hope, except it is more extreme and has become cosmic. The canvas for Israel's hope cannot be contained or domesticated within the historical process. It must be as comprehensive as is the lordly splendor of Yahweh.

(4) In both prophetic and apocalyptic texts we are presented with the overarching metaphor of biblical faith, namely, the kingdom of God, the rule of God, the ordering of life according to the purpose and will of God.[14] This hoped-for kingdom when God's will is fully visible will displace all the orderings and kingdoms of life that now claim our allegiance (Rev. 11:15).[15] The metaphor of the kingdom is a radical, revolutionary metaphor which stands in judgment over all the power arrangements presently available. The promised kingdom places all current arrangements in jeopardy. The coming of the new age and the new governance of God is at the heart of biblical faith. It has roots in the Sinai covenant which Buber has seen to be a radical political assertion. It is the overriding context of the prophets, who expect and insist that God's rule take public and visible form. The metaphor comes to its most poignant expression in the tradition around Jesus. His life and teachings embody that rule of God, evident in his teachings (Mark 1:14–15), in his acts (Luke 7:21–23), and in his parables. In response to this massive tradition of hope the church prays regularly that God's kingdom come on earth, as in heaven.[16]

(5) Finally, of the dimensions of biblical hope I will mention, both Jews and Christians wait for the *Messiah who is to come.* Too much time has been wasted on Jewish-Christian conflicts over this hope.[17] What matters is that Jews and Christians hold firmly to the conviction that one will come from God who will "mend the world." How and when and who that will be is not a proper issue for these convictions of hope. For the theme of hope, it does not matter greatly that Jews wait for a first coming and Christians wait for a second coming. Jews and Christians stand waiting together. At the center of that common faith is a contrast with the nonbelieving

world. That world does not wait for the Messiah but for Godot, who never comes. Against such despair these convictions of faith know about a coming one who precludes resignation and despair. Indeed, the worship and theology informed by these convictions are largely a reflection on that staggering concrete act of hope. That hope is a reading of history against the common reading which leads to hopelessness. But, because God oversees history, it is affirmed that present shapes of reality and power are all provisional, kept open for the other One, not yet here but very sure to come.

This catalog of biblical texts shows that hope belongs centrally and decisively to biblical faith. There is no way around it, if one takes the Bible seriously. These faith communities of Christians and Jews live in a passionate and profound hope that the world will become the world God intends, the world for which we yearn.

Viewed from the perspective of the dominant (and dominating) operating assumptions of our cultural context, the massive statement of hope contained in these texts seems foolish or, if not foolish, at best irrelevant. That is, it doesn't seem to touch the "real world" which appears so permanent. The promises belong to a different rationality and are presented precisely by poets and storytellers who operated (from our modern perspective) with a quite doubtful epistemology.

The dissonance in the juxtaposition of hope and reason needs to be taken seriously by us. The tradition of hope (Jewish-Christian faith) does not stand next to the tradition of reason (and science) in a chronological way, as though the hope tradition is primitive and has been superseded with the coming of modern knowledge. Nor is it the case that the tradition of hope can be bracketed out in a corner somewhere, as if it were a private religious mode separated off from the great public questions of power. The hope tradition is alive and addresses the realities of public life. It moves with an alternative reason of a different sort, which might be called "historical reason."[18]

The issue of the juxtaposition of hope and knowledge is at the heart of the crisis now to be faced in our culture. The traditions of *scientific knowledge and power* seem oddly alienated from the traditions of hope.[19] The tradition of hope means a relinquishment of control over life, not in the sense of life being out of control, but in the sense of governance being entrusted to this Holy One whom we cannot explain. This hope does not consist of losing control, but relinquishing it in trust.[20] It is thus an important question in our society about what happens if the managers of scientific knowledge can no longer entertain serious, concrete hope beyond our knowledge. Under such conditions, control becomes defensive and perhaps oppressive. The tradition of hope has its powerful say now among those cut off from scientific power and alienated by scientific norms of context. *The substance of biblical hope,* reflected in these texts, is a new world of justice, equity, freedom, and well-being. This hope has nothing to do with progress, for what is promised is wrought in inscrutable ways by the gift of the holy God where we least expect it.[21]

II

These biblical texts announce therefore that a better world of justice and equity is coming, as promised by God. The first issue raised by the tradition of hope is this. What is the function of hope? Why is hope practiced? What happens when a people hopes? The answer I make is: *hope keeps the present arrangement open and provisional.* Hope reminds us that the way things are (and all the extrapolations we make from that),[22] is precarious and in jeopardy. Hope reminds us not to absolutize the present, not to take it too seriously, not to treat it too honorably, because it will not last.

Because hope has such a revolutionary function, it is more likely that failure to hope—hopelessness—happens among the affluent, the prosperous, the successful, the employable, the competent, for whom the present system works so well. We are the ones who are likely to be seduced into taking the present political, economic, intellectual system too seriously and to equating it with reality. Indeed, it is prudent to take it that way, because that is where the jobs and benefits are. The more one benefits from the rewards of the system, the more one is enraptured with the system, until it feels like the only game in town and the whole game. Our "well-offness" leads us finally to absolutize, so that we may say "the system is the solution."[23] The system wants us to believe that, for such belief silences criticism. It makes us consenting, docile, obedient adults. The system wants to contain all our hopes and fears, wants us to settle for the available system of rewards.

We may say of the system's claim to absolutism: first, the system does not comprehend and benefit everyone and everything. There are always outsiders who are excommunicated and nullified and declared nonexistent. Every political system serves some at the cost of others. Every economic system benefits some at the expense of others. Every intellectual system eliminates the data and the people who do not fit. The urgent, unavoidable question then is: *what about those others?* What about the ones without access? Do they count? Are they bad? Are they nonpersons? We have a long history of denying their existence, the poor, women, Blacks, the handicapped, all kinds of disqualified people. The more rigorously the absolutizing works, the tighter they are locked out and the more of them there are who are locked out.

Second, biblical faith is suspicious of the system. It suggests that even those well inside the system should not expect too much. That is, even for its own adherents, the system finally cannot keep all its promises. So it is with the phone company; to say that the phone company is the solution to communications is surely not true, because communication is a human possibility and a human problem. This is not to say the phone company has no value, but is simply to say that systems in their hopelessness tend to make pretentious claims and run roughshod over those who doubt or resist. Such pretentious claims pushed to extremity become idolatry.

So what is the function of hope of this unreasonable, exotic kind? It is to provide standing ground *outside the system* from which the system can be evaluated, critiqued, and perhaps changed. Hopeless people eventually must conform, but hope-filled people are not as dependent, not as fully contained and administered. Hope is an immense human act which reminds us that no system of power or knowledge can finally grasp what is true. We must take care not to surrender our imaginative power to any pretension of absoluteness. Let me cite three examples of this critical function of hope.

(1) The text of Isaiah 55:1–5 is set in the sixth-century Exile,

when Jews were contained in the brutal Babylonian system of reality. Babylonian politics (Isa. 46) and Babylonian religion (Isa. 47) had largely claimed the day. In this context the Israelite poet issues an incredibly promissory statement:

> "Ho, every one who thirsts,
>   come to the waters;
> and he who has no money,
>   come, buy and eat!
> Come, buy wine and milk
>   without money and without price.
> Why do you spend your money for that which is not bread,
>   and your labor for that which does not satisfy?" (55:1–2)

The poet sets up a contrast between the "work bread" system of the empire and the "free food" system of the Israelite God. It is the memory of manna, of strangely given bread for the destitute, that becomes the ground of hope (cf. Exod. 16). This is not the offer of a production scheme, only an imaginative act of hope wrought in poetry. The poet lives toward a vision[24] and dares to think about a time to come when there will be no hunger because bread will be given for all. It is a fanciful, visionary assertion, the kind out of which new history is wrought.

Notice what this poem does. It permits a critique to be announced. The poetry is addressed to those without hope who had accepted Babylonian definitions of reality, who thought all of life was reduced to a single Babylonian definition. The poet invites Israelites to disengage their imagination from Babylonian shapes of reality. In fact, this poetry amounts to a delegitimation of Babylonian authority.[25] The power of poetic hope creates a way in which Israelites may have freedom of action, but the freedom of action apart from the all-consuming system depends on the *freedom of imagination* and speech done by the poet.[26] The hope of a different bread system permits and authorizes a critique of the empire.

(2) In Isaiah 65:17–25 the promissory vision of new heaven and new earth is an act of critical hope. This text is an eloquent statement of an alternative reality which is the substance of hope. It is the literature of a disenfranchised community which was oppressed by the dominant priesthood.[27] That priesthood so

controlled and preempted everything in terms of power, influence, and access that the minority group speaking in this poetry had its life nearly squeezed out. Isaiah 65 is the poetry of that minority which asserts an alternative mode of historical existence.

It is in a situation of marginality that the poet speaks. This act of hope, I submit, is not to be taken literally but poetically. The poem wants the oppressed group to have freedom of space and courage enough to act. Yet it could not do so as long as the absolute present prevailed. As long as the dominant group controlled everything, no one had power to act against it. This vision of new heaven, new earth, and new Jerusalem, however, invites the hopeless to act in a fresh way.

(3) The third example occurs in the book of Daniel. The book of Daniel is filled with extravagant hope against the tight system of royal reality. The symbol of oppressive political power is King Nebuchadnezzar, who may be taken to refer to any oppressive power.[28] That is, Nebuchadnezzar is symbol and model, not a historical person. He is presented as the paradigm of all totalitarian evil. In the narrative of 3:16–18 Nebuchadnezzar wants these model Jewish men, Shadrach, Meshach, and Abednego, to bow down. That is, he wants them to acknowledge the absolute claims of the imperial system, to concede the absolute authority of the system over their lives. These three Jews, though, are model practitioners of hope. They are so grounded in the liberation tradition of hope that they will not finally submit. They believe there is a future yet to be given that is not under the control of the king. The fact that their lives are grounded in the hope of a future given by God makes it possible for them to defy the system of Nebuchadnezzar. Out of their hope they offer this marvelous syllogism:

> O Nebuchadnezzar, we have no need to answer you in this matter. If it be so, our God whom we serve is able to deliver us from the burning fiery furnace; and he will deliver us out of your hand, O king. But if not, be it known to you, O king, that we will not serve your gods or worship the golden image which you have set up.

Their hope is a wonderful act of defiance. Perhaps we will be delivered. Perhaps not. Either way, we will not submit. Hope makes it possible not to submit. No wonder the response of the men fills the king with fury (3:19), because it signifies a dramatic end of his royal claims and his capacity to intimidate.

In all three cases, Isaiah 55 in exile against Babylon, Isaiah 65 against an oppressive priesthood, and Daniel 3 against Nebuchadnezzar, hope gives reason not to submit to present power arrangements. Hope affirms, in each case, that the present well-established power is not permanent and need not be taken with too much seriousness.

Herbert Schneidau has written an important book on Israel's historical perspective. His book has the telling title, *Sacred Discontent*,[29] which precisely captures Israel's perspective. Israel has a chronic discontent with the present. It is endlessly suspicious and refuses to accept the orders of the day. Schneidau labels this discontent "sacred" because it comes of God. This "sacred discontent" is rooted in *hope*. The hope is in the overriding power of God to work a new will against the order of the day. It is this act of hope which holds the present critically and loosely. Israel knows, in all these texts, that the purpose of God finally will move against the way things are. The function of this sacred discontent which is Israel's hope is to keep us from becoming excessively contented with the way things are.

III

The second issue emerging from these biblical texts of hope is: what is the *normal habitat of hope?* Who keeps the present open to new interventions from God and in what contexts? The hope tradition in ancient Israel suggests this answer: *hope emerges among those who publicly articulate and process their grief over their suffering.* That answer is an oddity, but it is more than an oddity. It is a great mystery that cuts to the heart of biblical faith. It is a fact of experience that violates all of our reasonable expectations. We would not expect hope to emerge especially and peculiarly among the ones who suffer.

At the outset, let us identify three places where hope is unlikely to appear with any power. First and most surprising, hope does not appear among the managers of the status quo. They may be optimists or progressives or evolutionists or developmentalists, but they are not the most likely to be ones who hope. People excessively committed to present power arrangements and present canons of knowledge tend not to wait expectantly for the newness of God.

In the historical narrative of Israel we may see this reality among the kings and priests, the managers of the status quo. Regularly these leaders are juxtaposed to the prophets who are the voices of hope in Israel. The prophets intend that priests and kings should listen and be open to the risk of the future, but characteristically they do not do so. Characteristically priests and kings seek to silence prophets and crush the voice of hope because they find this voice too threatening. We may cite King Ahab, who regarded Elijah as a "troubler" (1 Kings 18:17). We may refer to Amaziah, the royal priest who banishes the prophet Amos (Amos 7:10–17). We may observe the kings and governors a century later who want to execute Jeremiah (Jer. 26, 36) because he spoke a critical word which opened the present to the surprise of the future. The reaction of those in control to such a critical word of hope is to become defensive, to attempt to keep the future from impinging on the present in any serious way. Jeremiah (6:14; 8:11) sees this manipulative ploy. They say, "Shalom, shalom, well-being, well-being, peace and prosperity," when things are in fact not like that at all. Ezekiel (13:8–16) accuses the managers of the status quo of "whitewash," of covering over the incongruities and attempting to keep the system intact, even when that system has ceased to function. The managers (be they kings, priests, or false prophets) do not wait or expect or anticipate, because they believe that whatever comes next will be a diminishment of what they have now. Such people become adept at labels, crying "treason" (Jer. 38:4), "conspirator" (Amos 7:10), or "blasphemer" (Mark 2:7) against any who hope against the present. Finally, those who are excessively limited to the present ordering of things are hopeless.

Second and closely related, hope does not appear among the intellectuals who reflect on systems categories and expect nothing new from God. We might call this group statespersons, advisors, or even consultants. Their task in ancient Israel is to reflect on how things work, to make things work for their patrons.[30] These intellectuals think, shrewd as they are, in a closed, managed system. That system is clearly discernible in the book of Proverbs. Life is understood in terms of fixed cause-and-effect relationships. To be sure, life is not fully buttoned down, as there is always some inexplicable element,[31] but the technical explanation of the inexplicable is the main point of such an intellectual enterprise. It is the kind of knowledge a regime can live with and sponsor. Indeed, one would not expect in the book of Proverbs any radical statement of disruption, discontinuity, or hope. This sapiential outlook comes to its weary culmination in the book of Ecclesiastes which concludes that there really is no new thing, no ground for hope:

> All streams run to the sea,
>   but the sea is not full;
> to the place where the streams flow,
>   there they flow again. (Eccles. 1:7)
> What has been is what will be,
>   and what has been done is what will be done;
>   and there is nothing new under the sun. (Eccles. 1:9)

The present presumed world contains and accounts for everything.[32]

Third, hope does not appear among the oppressed silent sufferers. This argument is literally *an argument from silence*. That is, the people in bondage are so beaten down that they cannot utter a word. They cannot speak their hurt. They cannot articulate their grief and misery. I cite no texts, because these people give us no text. If we had a text for them, then they would have a voice. But they have no voice, so no text, and so no hope. That is why every totalitarian regime controls the media to keep others silent, stops the artists, and forbids assembly. People become dangerous voices of hope when they assemble or have a chance for solidarity, but if they can be kept mute they can be held in servility.

Hope is not likely to come then among royal managers, among hired intellectuals, or among the muted oppressed. Who hopes? Those who enter their grief, suffering, and oppression, who bring it to speech, who publicly process it and move through it and beyond. They are the ones who are surprised to find, again and again, that hope and new social possibility come in the midst of such grief (cf.

Rom. 5:3). Grief of that sort can be silenced from two sides, *from beneath* by those too beaten to cry and *from above* from those who see no pain.

The governing example of biblical hope is the Exodus narrative. That event is the primal act of hope in the Bible. Out of it comes a certitude that God will sooner or later bring justice and freedom into the world, even for slaves, even against empires. That certitude, however, was not arrived at easily. It arose from the oppressed people around Moses who made bricks for the empire. In the face of Pharaoh this people groaned. They cried out. They protested. They raged. They brought their common misery to public speech, which must have been an incredibly dangerous thing to do. Such common misery brought to public speech is a force in history that neither the tyrannical Pharaoh nor the great God above can ignore. It is written in this story of hope that "God heard their groaning, and God remembered his covenant. . . . And God saw the people of Israel, and God knew their condition" (Exod. 2:24–25). Suffering brought to speech concerns hope, because such protest in prayer and in public life is a refusal to let things be this way when they are in fact unbearable.

Out of that model event and that modeling narrative, we may extrapolate to our own time. The serious new hope for Blacks, women, and the handicapped in our time has come from *pain expressed*. It could come no other way. It was the long experience of pain and grief voiced that led to Martin Luther King, Jr.'s "I have a dream." It was the sisterhood come to voice that has brought hope to many depressed and immobilized women. It is rage made visible that has caused the handicapped to be given access and indeed noticed as present people. Indeed, if there is no grief brought to voice, there will be only *status quo,* only hopelessness, only invisibility, and therefore docility.

IV

The third issue emerging from these biblical texts of hope is: who are *the enemies of hope?* What works to keep hope from having power among us? I will suggest three aspects of an answer, which I judge to be clearly biblical and also clearly urgent in our contemporary scene.

(1) The first enemy of hope is *silence, civility, and repression.*[33] Where grief is denied and suffering is kept isolated, unexpressed, and unprocessed in a community, we may be sure hopelessness will follow. Silence may come because this sufferer lacks the courage or will to speak. But behind that, I submit, is *the long-term pressure from above.* The rulers of this age crave order above all. They have learned that silence is the way to preserve order, even if that order is unjust and dysfunctional. Where there is no speech about grief and suffering, there can be no hope.

In the New Testament, in Mark 10:46–52, there is a remarkable incident concerning the blind beggar, Bartimaeus. He waited along the road. When he heard that Jesus was coming, he began to cry out for help. He said, "Have mercy on me." He understood well the injunction, "Ask, and it will be given." He asked in the only way he knew how. The next line in the narrative is most surprising: "Many rebuked him, telling him to be silent." Do you wonder why? Because it was an embarrassment, a disruption, just not nice? Perhaps so. Or perhaps that is the only way one can administer beggars. If he were kept silent, he would remain hopeless and remain a docile beggar, but the narrative goes on to say, "He cried out all the more." He was not muted and therefore not hopeless. By the end of the story he has gained well-being, but he had to resist the pressure to be silent, or he would have had no chance, no hope.

(2) On the other side, the great enemy of hope is *fulfillment.* Scholars call this "realized eschatology." Good news tempts people to imagine that the promises are fully kept and the gifts already actualized. Thus, for example, Paul rebukes the Corinthians for their arrogance in presuming that their existence is the complete fulfillment of God's promise (1 Cor. 4:8). If *muteness* is a problem from below, obviously *fulfillment* is a problem from above, from the well-off who are satiated to boredom and cynicism, who have no want, desire nothing, and need only to protect what they already have. The narcotic power of fulfillment is evident in the parable of Luke 12:16–21 (cf. 1 Kings 4:20–21). "The land of a rich man brought forth plentifully." The line is overloaded with blessing. The

man had *land*. It was bottomland. He had a good crop. He could think only of storing the blessing. He said, "You have ample goods laid up for many years; take your ease, eat, drink, be merry." Abruptly he dies, prematurely. He dies, says the story, because he was poor toward God. When the present is coterminous with our best dreams, then there is no further dream, no vision toward which to live, and finally no hope.

(3) I am so bold as to suggest that the third enemy of hope is *technique*, the capacity to figure out, analyze, and problem-solve. I understand that people of hope cannot live without technique. For that reason, the relationship between hope and technique is a delicate and complex problem, and I do not oversimplify. But, because my theme is hope, I am driven to consider the ways in which technique may nullify hope. In the Bible, technique, the capacity to reduce life's mysteries to manageable, discrete elements, is embodied in the wise men of Pharaoh (Exod. 8) who are called magicians, in the wise men and magicians in the Joseph narrative (Gen. 41) who are to interpret dreams, in the wise men of Nebuchadnezzar who fail (Dan. 2), and in the religious experts who are condemned (Deut. 18:9–11), who manage the religious system. There may be other examples, but this is a fair sample. Notice the representatives of technique include both religious and secular political experts who believe that the data on hand will provide sufficient knowledge and power, when rightly read, to handle the future.

My comments in regard to hope and technique are not so much about knowledge as they are about a *sociology of knowledge*. That is, where do these technocrats live, how do they discern, and for whom? They tend to live in the patronage of the established order. Technique is never democratically distributed nor is its use neutral. It is always funded and sponsored by the "big house," and so, predictably, it is likely to serve those ends. Not only are the wise funded by the established patronage, but also the knowledge so derived is always in the interest of royal policy. Technique is never disinterested. Its interest is to domesticate and harness the future for "reasons of state."

These narratives are in the Bible because in each instance the expert of technique fails, and an outsider must be brought in. In each case (Moses, Joseph, Daniel) the outsider turns out to be a faithful Israelite, one who has no credentials but is grounded in hope and therefore has the capacity to gain life and give it. Perhaps the Bible means to be making something of an ironic statement on this subject to say that *the reality of power and knowledge* does not always cohere with *the forms of power and knowledge*. It is a question in Israel (and perhaps always) how the liberated power of hope and the careful administration of technique can live with each other.

V

The power of hope in the biblical texts focuses on these three issues which must be faced if we are to understand hope as more than religious escapism:

(1) The *function of hope* is to keep the present open and provisional, under scrutiny.

(2) The *natural setting of hope* is among those who have grief and process it in the community.

(3) The *enemies of hope* include muteness, fulfillment, and technique, all ways of trying to keep life on our own terms.

The capacity for hope is profoundly at issue in our society. Ours is a society in which hopelessness is prevalent and powerful. The power of hopelessness as a social force is extraordinary because the various enemies of hope are in a remarkable alliance. This includes:

(1) the mute servants (silent majority) who will never risk but always conform;

(2) the affluent who are satiated with fulfillment; and

(3) the bright ones with technique who inevitably are sponsored by the royal house.[34]

It is not fated that none of these should hope, but it is probable that none of these will hope. If that be so, then we are tempted into a deeper season of despair and hopelessness, reinforced both from above and from below. Despair does crazy things to us. The evidences of despair in our time include:

the action of *terrorists* which is a desperate, hopeless act of those without access or prospect of access to dignity or influence;

the posture of *conformity* among those who refuse to question but are ready to embrace and salute whatever turns out to be established official truth, both political and religious;

the temptation to *absolutize* in which critical capacity is routinely impossible in public life.

Temptations to terror, conformity, and absolutizing are all of a piece. They breed in contexts where there is no prospect of a future which will be different from the present.

Despair may be the critical fact of our common life. When we despair, we do crazy, inhumane, and ruthless things in the world, as is now widespread both publicly and domestically. This biblical tradition of hope stands as an alternative, an invitation to practice a critical dream, but that alternative requires a certain disengagement, a certain risky imagination. The people gathered around the biblical texts of hope practice that risky imagination from time to time. It begins in not eating at the king's table (Dan. 1). Eating at the king's table invites despair. An alternative diet of manna makes hope possible and powerful.

king's table or manna?

5

Will Our Faith
Have Children?

I want to consider the claims of evangelical faith around the biblical metaphor of children. In 1976 John Westerhoff asked, *Will Our Children Have Faith?*[1] By this he meant: will we transmit our faith to the next generation? Undoubtedly this is an important and serious question. My title plays on that theme and seeks to turn it around: will our faith have children? Such a theme might mean with Westerhoff: will there be a next generation which still believes? Or it might cut below that to ask: will there be a next generation at all? Is there a future, given the precarious reality of our human community in a nuclear age? In that context the crucial question is not even the survival of faith but the survival of the children. I intend, however, to cut below that as well to ask: will we be open enough, risking enough, vulnerable enough, that God may give us a future that we do not plan or control or contrive? By the question, "Will our faith have children?" I mean to ask: are we open enough to receive a future from God which will surprise us? It is assumed in evangelical faith that any real future is given us underived, unextrapolated, ex nihilo, by the mercy of God (cf. 1 Cor. 4:7).

I

The Old Testament is much occupied with the securing of an heir, with the reception of a seed for the future which assures that our present generation is not the last one. That, of course, is the main theme of the Abraham-Sarah narrative, but the affirmative use of the metaphor of a future child is most poignant in Isaiah 54:1–3:

> "Sing, O barren one, who did not bear;
>   break forth into singing and cry aloud,
>   you who have not been in travail!
> For the children of the desolate one will be more
>   than the children of her that is married, says the LORD.
> Enlarge the place of your tent,
>   and let the curtains of your habitations be stretched out;
> hold not back, lengthen your cords
>   and strengthen your stakes.
> For you will spread abroad to the right and to the left,
>   and your descendants will possess the nations
>   and will people the desolate cities."

The community of believers was in exile. They were without resources, cut off from Jerusalem and the temple, doubtful of God's power, enmeshed in a Babylonian lifeworld that shaped everything in ways alien to them. They had no prospect of a way out, no hope for a next generation. They had no continuing city, no abiding structures, no enduring myths. They were bereft of possibility. (No wonder that great evangelical preacher of the sixteenth century wrote about the "Babylonian captivity of the church"!)

The poet of Isaiah 54 wants to announce a fresh, inexplicable intervention of God which will liberate, permit homecoming, and evoke the anticipated community of obedience. Isaiah uses many poetic devices but none more astonishing than the metaphor of the children. The barren one will have children. The barren one is

Sarah (Gen. 11:30), Rebekah (Gen. 25:21), Rachel (Gen. 29:30), and Hannah (1 Sam. 1:2). Ours is a community of barren women and unproductive men (cf. Heb. 11:12) with no possibility of creating a future of their own. The barren one in this poem is exiled Israel as well as the church whenever it reaches the end of its resources, which is often and soon and surely now.

Precisely to the barren one is the promise made, "Sing barren one, you who have not been in labor." Rejoice because from barrenness issues a new generation which will outreach the married, full, affluent, technologically secure Babylon. The statement is nonsensical unless it is taken as evangelical, i.e., hope against the reason of the day. The same reality is given in Exodus when the Israelite women with their midwives terrified the empire with their many births (Exod. 1:17–22). The births are inexplicable, caused only by the powerful graciousness of God who will work a newness when all is lost. Isaiah 54 draws on a similar domestic, intimate metaphor, but the domestic metaphor, of course, has political and public freight, as the emperor always recognizes. The domestic metaphor concerns the dismantling of all imperial forms of life. It offers the strange calculus of God's weakness being strong, of God's foolishness being wise, of the humbled ones being exalted in their call (cf. 1 Cor. 1:26). Isaiah 54 is an utterly absurd, unscientific poem which embarrasses our technical reason and must have embarrassed those Jews in exile who had compromised with Babylonian modes of reality. A newness not scheduled in any of the social scientific grids of the day is hardly cause for reorganization and departing, unless of course the listening community makes a break in its reason.

The metaphor is pursued in Isaiah 54 with a marvelously playful picture. Stronger tent pegs and tent cords are now required because the peasant abode will be crawling with children, spreading abroad, seizing the land, reoccupying the city, no doubt terrifying the emperor as previously done to the Pharaoh. The force unleashed in this poetic promise brings to nought the things that are (1 Cor. 1:28). Poetic metaphor must be used to speak these things, because no other language is adequate to the radical, surely irrational inversion of the world.[2]

II

This poem looks forward as well as backward. The metaphor in Isaiah 54:1–3 serves the church well. Paul is driven to the edge of his considerable intellectual gifts to express the wonder of the gospel. In his letter to the Galatians he wants to characterize the stultifying life of knuckling under to the rulers of this age, which leads to numbness and finally to despair. That Paul is able to do, but when he comes to characterize the evangelical alternative, his reasonable words fail. As elsewhere, at this moment of central affirmation Paul must break back into poetry. How remarkable that this new situation with this fresh first-century crisis point is drawn to the same sixth-century poem, reiterated in Galatians 4:27 (author's translation):

> "Rejoice, O barren one that dost not bear;
>   break forth and shout, thou who art not in travail;
> for the desolate hath more children
>   than she who hath a husband."

Again the issue is not Sarah and Hagar, but it is also not Babylon and exile as in Isaiah 54. Now it is the scribal consciousness which cannot receive the newness of the gospel.

Paul is fascinated with the birth metaphor, because it is a way to speak of the unutterable, inexplicable gift. In Galatians 4:19 he can write, "My little children, with whom I am again in travail until Christ be formed in you!" That text suggests a growth of the embryo of Christ in the body of believers. In Romans 8:22–23 Paul characterizes the whole world as being in painful labor for the redemption of our bodies.

This theological tradition derived from Second Isaiah and Paul refuses to absolutize either the Babylonian order (in the sixth century) or the rule of positive law (in the first century). Our theological tradition, radical as it is, does not absolutize the present contrived economic arrangement, because there is a groaning and a time to come when our bodies will be redeemed and when there will be an end to alienated work. Our theological tradition, radical as it is, does not absolutize any intellectual scheme, any closed system of signs that imagines all the truth is given and all the judgments already rendered. We treasure this free mother Sarah, who is bound in freedom only for the fruits of the Spirit (Gal. 5:22). Mother Sarah stands as a metaphor for the possibilities given to us that lie beyond our contriving and conjuring, the only source of new children.

III

Talk about newness is easy, however, easier than the reality of newness. Our talk must not be easy or glib. Israel knows that as well. We do remember former things (cf. Ps. 137:4–6). We remember them partly because we covet the wrong things and do not want to relinquish, but also because we cherish the right things and properly linger. Isaiah 54:1–3 and Galatians 4:27 are an invitation to move beyond all present arrangements and let life be shattered for God's new act of life (above all, see Isa. 43:18–19). Israel does not speak easily of new life. It knows new life is given in pain and with great cost.

The main point I wish to argue about evangelical faith is this: Second Isaiah could not announce the new birth until there had been two generations of Jeremiah to grieve the loss. The other side of evangelical faith, the first side of the dialectic which claims us, is the pathos-filled speech of Jeremiah 31:15:

> Thus says the LORD:
> "A voice is heard in Ramah,
>   lamentation and bitter weeping.
> Rachel is weeping for her children;
>   she refuses to be comforted for her children,
>   because they are not."[3]

Will our faith have children indeed! It has already had them—and lost them.

The rhetoric of Jeremiah takes us to the ashheap of burnt Jerusalem. The prophet saw the burnt temple, the charred city walls. He observed the absence of the royal court. He named the names of those carried away to Babylon. He took note of the brutality of the Babylonian armies, the damage done even to civilians, to unvalued women and innocent children. The sweep of imperial death takes all. The Deuteronomists might have explained it all as deserved punishment, given a stern system of retribution. The task of poets, however, is to cut underneath such conventional certitudes and discern the human cost and the human hurt. Those killed in 587, as in any such holocaust, were neither numbers in a simple calculus nor statistics in the nightly news in Babylon. They were named, loved children. They had mothers and fathers who cared for them and who called them for supper (and they did not answer). Second Isaiah may delight in the labor room of new possibility, but we must not delight to go there too soon. We linger at the morgue over the charred bodies which can scarcely be identified. We grieve over them because they are the treasured children, the only future we shall ever have, now brutally become past, irreversible past. We know also that we shall never have any others, only these, so we flinch from the question too easily put: will our faith have children?

> "Rachel is weeping for her children,
> she refuses to be comforted for her children,
> because they are not." (Jer. 31:15)

Evangelical faith is not escape to a naive, never-never land. There are pseudoforms of evangelical faith which move easily to the next triumph and the next wave of the future,[4] but serious evangelical faith is of another kind. It is as concrete as today, as specific as Rachel, as vulnerable as these little bodies. It is indignant with rage over the inhumanity. The true evangelicals are those whose eyes notice the hurt and whose noses smell the grief. Jeremiah is a poet of faith who has himself battled God but now is free enough of his own agenda to look beyond self and to notice those in his world crushed by the rapacious system, destroyed by self-seeking, and stunned by the very cut of steel against baby fat. The crying which Jeremiah imagines is for the children and only incidentally for the governors of such a deathly system and the religious ones who pray over it (cf. Luke 19:41–44).

No word of comfort must be spoken now. It is a mockery to

comfort. Nobody is as irrelevant in such a moment of reality as is Second Isaiah with his buoyant, hopeful poem. Not wrong, just grossly inappropriate.

IV

Jeremiah of course stands deep in tradition in this moment of pathos. Rachel learned how to cry this way because she had been wife to this husband Jacob, whose life is one of pathos. We are not in the grand symmetrical tranquillity of Abraham, who never seemed to be bothered and who, with Sarah, laughed (cf. Gen. 17:17; 18:12; 21:6). We are in the rage-filled, incongruous world of Jacob and Rachel, who know conflict and cunning, who value life in its raw gift and are not given to grand speculation or noble faith. This generation always lives at the eleventh hour of precariousness —and now "they are not."

Now with father Jacob, Rachel is dead. There will be no more children. Jacob treasures the ones he has. Then in Genesis 37 (after Rachel is dead [Gen. 35:19–20] and the faith will have no more children), enter the older brothers who are filled with rage. For good reason they despise the beloved Joseph. They must lie to their father, and so they bring the beloved son's blood-covered robe. Jacob believes them, to his deep grief. The narrative catches the mood of death and grief (Gen. 37:35): "All his sons and all his daughters rose up to comfort him; but he refused to be comforted, and said, 'No, I shall go down to Sheol to my son, mourning.' " He refused to be comforted. He was not comforted until he held his grown precious son in his arms (Gen. 46:29–30). The one who was lost is found, was dead and is alive (cf. Luke 15:24). But until that inexplicable moment, Jacob refused to be comforted. No spiritual assurance, no neighborly acts, no piety, no religious or mythic continuities would matter. The father pushed that all away and embraced the dark rawness where God's promises seem not to extend. Rachel in 587 (Jer. 31:15), so long afterwards but with poignant, painful memory, now echoes Jacob, with the important difference that as yet there is no restoration. The children are gone. Rachel also asks, "Will our faith have children?" Yet she knows the heavy answer: it is "No." The grief is for loss, for hopelessness, for a future that is closed. Only the glib can say "Yes" in the face of Babylonian brutality.

Rachel in her grief looks both ways. She looks back to Jacob, who will not be comforted for his beloved Joseph. Rachel also looks forward and even there, nothing is changed. Matthew can write of the brutality of Herod, who tries to eliminate the gospel by killing the boy babies:

> Then was fulfilled what was spoken by the prophet Jeremiah:
> "A voice was heard in Ramah,
> wailing and loud lamentation,
> Rachel weeping for her children;
> she refused to be consoled,
> because they were no more." (Matt. 2:17–18)

Herod wants to make sure that the faith has no children, because the only sure way to preserve the old order is to be sure this faith yields no children. The deathly truth is that Herod and Rachel are united in this moment in believing that there will be no children for the faith. That Herod draws that conclusion is one more act of self-serving brutality. Rachel reaches the same conclusion in deep chagrin and grief.

V

An evangelical structuring of biblical faith, then, can be understood around the metaphor of children, a metaphor about openness to God's surprise. I have tried to suggest two shapings of the motif. One motif is *the ecstasy of surprising birth,* deriving from Sarah, used by Paul, but focusing on *the exile-ending lyrics of Isaiah 54:1–3.* The other motif is *grieving for lost children,* looking back to father Jacob in Genesis, looking toward Herod and the slaughter of precious, not just innocent, but precious children, and focusing on *the exile-embracing lament of Jeremiah 31:15.*

These two texts and their related clusters of texts provide ways of giving answer to our question, "Will our faith have children?" Isaiah 54 answers vigorously, joyously, unambiguously, "Yes." The poet evokes the faith of exiles with freedom enough to go home

(52:11–12), to relinquish imperial connections, to celebrate the rule of the liberating God in the face of Babylonian claims (46:1–4), to eat free bread in the face of coercive bread (55:1–3). The faith of those exiles will have children, abundant generations of heirs freely given, unimagined, uncontrived, given by the generosity of God, far more abundantly than we ask or think (cf. Eph. 3:20).

On the other hand, the pathos-filled word of Jeremiah also faces the question, "Will our faith have children?" Jeremiah, I suspect (and Rachel with him), would have been appalled not at the answer of Second Isaiah, but at the senselessness of the question. How dare anyone ask for new children or hope for them, for don't you know about the loss of children, the precious children, the only children (cf. Gen. 22:2)? We do not hope and dare not hope for new children or different children, because these lost children are the only children. For these we must refuse to be comforted. The question about such a new future is thus rather irrelevant and evokes no interest in the generation that knows the loss.

Emil Fackenheim has noticed a shrewd thing about Job.[5] In the first chapter (1:2–3) and in the last chapter (42:12–13) of Job, what he had at the beginning is nicely contrasted with what he had at the end. In all things but one, everything is precisely doubled at the restoration: from 7,000 sheep to 14,000 sheep; from 3,000 camels to 6,000 camels; from 500 yoke of oxen to 1,000 yoke of oxen; from 500 she-asses to 1,000 she-asses. In all things save one, Job has been doubly blessed. At the beginning he has seven sons and three daughters. At the end he has precisely seven sons and three daughters. They have not been multiplied or doubled. The number of children is the only number taken seriously, for children, the wave of our future, are precious, nonclonable, irrepeatable, concrete, and irreversible. So concrete are they at the end that the daughters are named, which sets them even beyond the sons.

Evangelical faith is not only *buoyant about new gifts* surprisingly given. Evangelical faith is also *candid and unflinching about hurt, loss, grief, and endings* in human history which are real and painful and not covered over. The concrete embrace of deep death is as evangelical as is the lyrical celebration of new gift. The answer to our question must, therefore, not be made lightly, easily, unambiguously, or with excessive buoyancy.

The key problem of our faith is how to relate continuity and discontinuity.[6] We ask whether the buoyant continuities cancel out and nullify the grief. How strange that when we engage in such affirmations we are at the same time deep into the hurt and rage that is not nullified. That is the problem of faith and that is the discernment now made about our Enlightenment self-deception, that our ways of transcending trouble may *suppress* but do not *nullify*. The critical problem that belongs to our question is how to relate the *pathos of Jeremiah* to the *buoyancy of Second Isaiah*.

It is clear enough, I judge, that Second Isaiah knew of the poetry of Jeremiah. When he uttered the triumphant note of Isaiah 54:1–3, he surely had not forgotten the pathos of Jeremiah 31:15. The connection between the two texts is evident in the general theme. The connection is not only thematic but is also evident in a common verbal usage.[7] Thus Jeremiah 31:19 reads:

> "I was ashamed [*bōštî*], and I was confounded [*niklamtî*],
> because I bore the disgrace [*ḥerpath*] of my youth [*nᵉ'ûrî*]."

Isaiah 54:4 reads:

> "Fear not, for you will not be ashamed [*tēbôšî*];
> be not confounded [*tikkālmî*], . . .
> for you will forget the shame [*bōšeth*] of your youth [*ᵃlûmayik*],
> and the reproach [*ḥerpath*] of your widowhood."

The Isaiah passage appears to be a quite deliberate and intentional response to the nullification of the Jeremiah text. (Ezek. 36:32, which also uses *bôš* and *kālam*, may be a middle expression between the Jeremiah and Isaiah passages.) Perhaps the key issue of evangelical faith, i.e., good news to exiles, is caught in how one can speak such a promise with full recognition of and respect for the loss and hurt already on the table. The promise of Isaiah 54:1–3 can follow the loss of Jeremiah 31:15 in several ways.

First, it is possible to take the point *chronologically*, a possibility not without merit. The grief of Jeremiah and of Rachel had been full and had spent itself, for time does indeed heal. Two long generations had passed. Grief finally does reach its bottom.[8] When it has reached that point, a new good word is permissible, even if not too soon. Possibly this bottoming in exilic Israel is aided by the reality of the poetry of the book of Lamentations, which is undoubtedly lodged between these two poets.[9] The way to move from Jeremiah to Second Isaiah is by way of Lamentations, which gives full range to the loss. It is there that Israel goes the full way to the bottom and then begins to move out. The links between Lamentations and Second Isaiah are still to be traced, but I have no doubt that the theme of "Comfort, comfort" (Isa. 40:1) is an intentional response to "none to comfort" (Lam. 1:2, 9, 17, 21). The newness of Isaiah 43:18–19 may also be triggered by the anticipated newness of Lamentations 3:22–23. Moreover the historical changes in the period, from Babylon to Persia (specifically Cyrus), permit a new word of hope.

Second, it is possible that we should take these texts not chronologically but *dialectically,* i.e., read them as theological statements informing and correcting each other, rather than as historical statements following in a single sequence. To an evangelical Christian reading from the dialectic of Good Friday and Easter, such a way has considerable merit.[10] Thus Israel knows too much to answer our question only with the lyric of Isaiah 54; it must always answer with both *grief and surprise,* and neither must supersede or nullify the other.

One may, however, read the move from Jeremiah to Second Isaiah in still another way. The unmitigated grief of Rachel is the parlance of hope. The grief of Israel is the only arena in which God's newness appears. The grief is to be neither chronologically superseded nor dialectically corrected, but rather is the experiential matrix wherein newness must be born if it is to be birthed at all. In the moment of such grief the deep groans are uttered wherein the revealing of the children of God can happen, there and nowhere else (Rom. 8:19). It has been so since the beginning of our people in Exodus 2:23–25. Paul, who knows so much about these two evangelical poets, learns with them that it is precisely suffering— embraced and practiced and articulated—that produces hope (Rom. 5:3–4). Suffering peculiarly produces hope like nothing else, but it must be suffering brought to speech in faithful ways.

Second Isaiah knows that. The barren Sarah—it could have been barren, bereaved Rachel—is addressed in the same chapter 54:

O afflicted one, storm-tossed, and not comforted. (vs. 11)

Sarah, exiled Israel, is also "not comforted," as Rachel is not in Jeremiah 31:15. It is precisely the one "not comforted," the one "refusing to be comforted," who has the chance of comfort. It is Rachel, whose troubled voice we hear all through the book of Lamentations, who finally is reached by this poet with the words, "Comfort, comfort my people." These poets and this people know that, in the person of Sarah, Rachel is also present.

Exegetically we come therefore to the answer, "Yes, our faith will have children." Our faith will not have children, though, if it imagines it can hold on to the old ones. Our faith will not have children if we glibly rush to newness. Also our faith will not have children if we imagine we can merely move from strength to strength, from children to children, and simply balance things off. It is indelibly written in our tradition that our children, i.e., our future from God, are given only when we linger long over the loss. Lingering long and honestly over the loss is foundational for newness. Elie Wiesel has observed how strange it is that the survivors of the Holocaust are precisely the ones who can yet believe in this God of pathos.[11] The other Jews who have not been into such hurt doubt more easily. It is not different with us Christians, who must be suspicious of those who easily promise new children without grief.

VI

The glib hope of new children without grief is a powerful temptation for our culture, an issue for those of us who are accustomed to having our way promptly about everything. The urgent pastoral task is to nurture people into an honest embrace of loss which our culture seeks to deny with phony promises and ersatz continuities.

In this connection two recent studies provide concrete examples of our inability to embrace loss. Alexander and Margarete Mitscherlich,[12] following Freud's study of melancholy, have considered the National Socialist movement in Germany and have found important roots in the German response to the losses of 1918 and Versailles. They suggest that the movement of Hitler is in part rooted in the inability to mourn. Because of that inability, society engaged in an enormous act of denial with all the religion needed to make it legitimate.

Closer home, Robert Jay Lifton[13] has studied American responses to the nuclear threat. He suggests our cultural situation is one in which there is

> an inability to believe in larger connections, by pervasive expressions of psychic numbing. These states can be directly manifested in various kinds of apathy, unrelatedness, and general absence of trust or faith; or more indirectly in social, artistic, and political struggles to break out of that numbing.[14]

He goes on to argue that the inability to mourn is part of a general breakdown in the symbolizing process, a form of dislocation in which experience is formless and chaotic. The response to such an inability is deadening self-indulgence of rank, individualism, or authoritarianism.

The studies of the Mitscherlichs and Lifton reveal in a paradigmatic way the pathology of our culture. I have settled on this theme of new children and loss of children because I believe the issue of discontinuity (loss and newness) concerns the ministry of the church in overriding ways. Our refusal or inability to face these issues of loss and newness leads to a diminishment of our humanity and generates an intense brutality among us. This failure at candor over our loss concerns the ministry of the church because there is so much fraudulent religion that denies and deceives. That religious temptation may come in fake evangelicalism which tells what we want to hear with shameless certitude, or it may appear as rational mysticism which screens out the historical, public issues. We are tempted in such ways of fake evangelicalism and rational mysticism in our theological tradition.

This failure to grieve and then to receive newness concerns the

ministry of the church because those of us who purport to be
genuinely evangelical are entrusted precisely with the resources and
discernments which could matter. It is my judgment that what our
culture now urgently needs is indeed what is entrusted to us. What is
needed is the honesty to relinquish and the courage to receive.
Evangelical faith is gifted precisely with the news about dying and
being raised. An evangelical ministry must fly in the face of most of
the ideology of our time, secular and religious, for this subversive
poetic tradition knows that Second Isaiah (with Sarah) could
rejoice only after Jeremiah (with Rachel) has refused to be
comforted.

VII

How are we finally able to answer the question, "Will our
faith have children?" Walker Percy[15] distinguishes between
knowledge/news available "on the island" and news from "across
the sea," i.e., disclosure that intrudes from outside our system but
which is urgent for us. To answer the question, "Will our faith have
children?" requires not just knowledge which is everywhere true,
not just news from the island of our habitation, but also news from
across the sea.

First, if I have rightly articulated an evangelical discernment of
reality, we must think about the abrasive interface between that
discernment and the dominant values in American society. We
experience and practice the American dream as a rush too easily
taken toward new children, bright tomorrows, more security, and
new energy resources, all within reach. We are smitten with
progress as a rational possibility so that we miss the hurt and grief.
Such unreal expectations are given us in political terms and in much
of establishment religion.

One never knows about the signs of the times, but there is
reason to think that the metaphor of dismantling in 587 B.C.E., to
which Jeremiah addressed himself, is not alien to where we may be
headed culturally. There is reason to think we now face a great
disappointment and a deep loss.[16] One can surmise that the
desperate move to put the wagons in a circle reflects the sense of

danger now common to us: that the American dream we have lived is precarious, if not ending. It helps very little to offer technological or religious certitudes that cushion the break.

The church's ministry is not only prophetic, to *note the ending,* but also pastoral, to *embrace the ending,* for with our fading historical position of dominance we may have as much to grieve about as does Rachel. Surely songs are to be sung about new children to the barren one. Initially, however, the loss, the grief, and the barrenness must be faced fully, and we may not be very skillful (cf. Amos 5:16) or willing to face them (Amos 6:6). Our propensity is to deny, cover up, and supersede the loss.

Second, I suggest this mode of evangelical faith requires a new look at what we are about in theological education. As Robert Lynn has observed, seminaries have become compatible with cultural dreams which are not really or fundamentally out of our theological tradition. We shall, by choice or necessity, have the opportunity to rethink that compatibility in the next few years. Seminaries may rightly grieve for times and children once treasured but now gone. If exile comes to the faithful church, the seminary is no place in which to be safe from it. We may not order our life as an immunity from the loss. Perhaps the seminary also has been a place of too much certitude, ready to sing before we grieve over our own deep ambiguity. Perhaps the seminary too easily embraces the norms of the academy, because it is easier to follow the right forms than to face the raw substance never fully caught in form. Perhaps the seminary has come to terms too fully with economic sufficiency, when members of the seminary—faculty, students, and board—count too much on treasures that comfort the heart. (That also is a measure of our enmeshment.) Perhaps the seminary has become too nearly a collection of "autonomous" believers, endlessly fascinated with ourselves and not very good at being the body of the one Lord. The voice of Rachel may be an imperative voice for our future.

Third, if culture must face the loss, if theological education might relinquish in order to receive, then what of the church constituency we dare to call evangelical? This church may in time to come recall with relief and gratitude that we are not summoned to be an echo of culture, either to admire its economics, to embrace its psychology, or to certify its morality. We are permitted an alternative way (cf. 1 Cor. 12:31—13:13) which to some will appear subversive and to others a more excellent way and to some both subversive and excellent. The faithful church is not called to replicate dangerous things of another generation, but is being led to the danger peculiar to our time. None of us knows what that might mean. Yet what a difference to have a church aware of the danger that comes with the loss of children and future, expectant that the loss will be embraced, ready to enter places where we have not been, wanting finally to sing of new children and new future which are surely to come, but not too soon.

If we choose ultimately to be that evangelical, there are of course many ways in which penultimately we continue the old ways. Penultimately, we shall be a culture that continues to seek order, security, and prosperity, but we shall have an open edge toward the harder, more demanding human issues of justice and humaneness. Penultimately, theological schools will continue to seek academic excellence and financial well-being, but we shall have an open edge toward the harder, more demanding faith questions of passion in a sea of apathy and of community in a torrent of individualism. Penultimately, we shall be a church that continues to seek growth, influence, and respectability, but we shall have an open edge toward the harder, more demanding evangelical questions of faithfulness, renewal, and information. Penultimate continuities for our culture, for the seminary, and for the church, are not to be mocked or treated lightly. Ultimately, however, our vocation calls us to notice the costs of those continuities, costs in terms of repression, denial, self-deception, and exploitation, costs which finally we are called not to pay. We are called with precious gifts and peculiar discernment, with odd power and access, to be present to the discontinuities where the new children are given in faith. Such birth is in mighty and painful labor. The children, who are given to us new by faith, never arrive in an easy birth, but it is the birth for which we wait in eager longing (Rom. 8:19–23).

The news of future children inexplicably given by the mercy of God is indeed the gospel. We may therefore sing the song of doxological discontinuity in which we are startled by gift. We are a community that believes our faith has a future. For it to be a future grounded in God's grief, however, it cannot be a future filled with deception or cover-up, pretense or denial, numbness or old habits. The future of our faith is a new future given precisely for us when we fully grieve that the old is lost and gone. The future is given to us by the God known fully in Jesus Christ, crucified and risen. Of that One, Rachel, utterly bereft, weeps on Friday and Sarah, utterly stunned, sings on Sunday.

Notes

Introduction

1. These issues have been carefully probed by James Barr, *The Scope and Authority of the Bible* (Explorations in Theology 7; London: SCM, 1980), especially in the first and third essays. Barr's move from "history" to "story" is congenial to my focus on "narrative events."
2. I take the notion of "following the narrative" from W. B. Gallie, "The Historical Understanding," *History and Theory,* ed. George H. Nadel (Middletown, CT: Wesleyan University, 1977) 149–202. I suggest that biblical modes of hope depend primarily on the capacity to follow the narrative.

Chapter 1

1. The basic work is that of James W. Fowler, *Stages of Faith* (San Francisco: Harper & Row, 1981). See also his more recent discussion, *Becoming Adult, Becoming Christian* (San Francisco: Harper & Row, 1984).
2. Jacob Neusner, "Judaism within the Disciplines of Religious Studies: Perspectives on Graduate Education," *Bulletin of the Council on the Study of Religion* 14:5 (December 1983) 143, has rightly asserted that there is finally only the study of a specific religion, not a general study of religions. Each must be considered in its substantive peculiarity.
3. On the Exodus narrative as the "core" of Israel's faith, see Walter Harrelson, "Life, Faith, and the Emergence of Tradition," *Tradition and Theology in the Old Testament,* ed. Douglas A. Knight (Philadelphia: Fortress, 1977) 11–30.
4. On the recurring power of such literature apart from the original event, see David Tracy, *The Analogical Imagination* (New York: Crossroad, 1981) 102 and passim.

5. Michael Fishbane, *Text and Texture* (New York: Schocken Books, 1979) 121–40, well expresses the continuing power of the text. Elie Wiesel, *Souls on Fire* (New York: Summit, 1971) 167–68, has made familiar to us the rabbinic teaching that if one cannot remember how to light the fire, how to say the prayer, how to find the place, it is sufficient to tell the story. The telling of the story is taken and received in this community as an act of transformed redescription. On the continuing revolutionary power of the Exodus narrative, see Michael Waltzer, *Exodus and Revolution* (New York: Basic, 1985).

6. On the character of the text in its "how" as revelatory, see Gail R. O'Day, "Irony and the Johannine Theology of Revelation: An Investigation of John 4" (Unpublished Dissertation, Emory University, 1983). See her further development of this theme forthcoming from Fortress, *Revelation in the Fourth Gospel: Narrative Mode and Theological Claim.*

7. Robert Coles, "Psychology as Faith," *Theology Today* 42 (1985) 69–71, has protested in most polemical fashion against the reduction of human questions to a psychological dimension. He explicitly names "stages of faith" as an example of this reductionism.

8. The capacity of the narrative mode to articulate the breakpoints is at the heart of current interest in narrative theology. The larger epistemological question, however, concerns the different modes of the social sciences, which are by definition descriptive, and the possibilities of literature to move beyond description, which is inherently conservative, to acts of liberation and imagination beyond present arrangements. Both in Scripture study and in understandings of human personality these epistemological matters dictate that how we speak, i.e., the categories used, is as important as what we say.

9. Thus Johannes Metz can speak of biblical narratives as "dangerous stories" because they subvert present social reality. See Thomas W. Ogletree, *Hospitality to the Stranger* (Philadelphia: Fortress, 1985) 5, where he speaks of the social transformation that happens when there are "courageous people daring to share forbidden tales."

10. On the enduring function of the classic, see the classical statement of Tracy, *The Analogical Imagination,* 102 and passim.

11. Susan Handelman, *The Slayers of Moses* (Albany: State University of New York, 1982), finds compelling evidence in the Jewish tradition that the "letter" does not kill, but indeed gives life. Her analysis of the Christian-Western yearning to "escape from textuality" is one that must be taken most seriously, even if it is a threat to our way of thinking. We have to reconsider the ways in which the text is concerned for transformation.

12. The phrase is that of Peter L. Berger and Thomas Luckmann, *The Social Construction of Reality* (Garden City, NY: Doubleday, 1966).

13. This is not to suggest that this literature lacks psychological sophistication but that its sophistication tends to be dramatic rather than analytic. My impression is that, as personality theory moves toward ego-construction theories as in the work of Robert Kegan, *The Evolving Self: Problems and Process in Human Development* (Cambridge: Harvard University, 1982), it moves from an analytic to a dramatic frame of reference. In doing so, its categories become more congruent with the narrative and liturgic presentations of the biblical literature.

14. See my discussion of covenant, "Covenanting as Human Vocation," *Interpretation* 33 (1979) 115–29. On interiority and interaction, see my study of David, *David's Truth* (Philadelphia: Fortress, 1985), especially chapter 2. See the use Fowler, *Becoming Adult, Becoming Christian*, 92–106, has made of the category of covenant in relation to faith development.

15. On the Exodus narrative as liturgic paradigm, see the normative study by Johannes Pedersen, *Israel III–IV* (London: Oxford University, 1940) 728–37.

16. See Brueggemann, *The Creative Word* (Philadelphia: Fortress, 1982) chapter 2. On the problematic between the generations in the transmission process, see Michael Fishbane, *Text and Texture*, 79–83.

17. Norman K. Gottwald, *The Tribes of Yahweh* (Maryknoll, NY: Orbis, 1979) 63–125, has shown the partisan character of these traditions.

18. A parallel may be found in the old slave South, so well explicated by Eugene D. Genovese, *Roll, Jordan, Roll* (New York: Pantheon, 1974). In a genuinely oppressed community, it would be unthinkable that the young would or could be protected from that overriding social reality. The children necessarily must be taught where the limits of defiance are, how to survive, and most of all, the proper anger that goes with oppression. Perhaps it is only our bourgeois perspective that leads us to want to protect the young and to extend innocence about our social reality. One way in which this is done is to imagine that only "nice" Bible stories can be used.

19. See Paul Ricoeur, "The Critique of Religion," *The Philosophy of Paul Ricoeur*, ed. Charles E. Reagan and David Stewart (Boston: Beacon, 1978) 213–22, on demystification and demythologization as dimensions of suspicion. A fuller statement of the meaning of suspicion is expressed in *Freud and Philosophy* (New Haven: Yale University, 1970).

20. See Herbert N. Schneidau, *Sacred Discontent: The Bible and Western Tradition* (Baton Rouge: Lousiana State University, 1977), who finds this inclination definitional to a biblical perception of reality.

21. Genovese, *Roll, Jordan, Roll,* concludes that the Black slaves survived with dignity and humaneness because they were clear that they did not

finally belong to the white world. That certitude was sustained by
regular and intentional liturgical processing which told the truth about
the world of Black people. On p. 251, speaking of Black religion he
writes: "the idea of Heaven, with its equality before God, gives them a
strong sense of what they are destined to become. It thereby introduces
a sense of worth and reduces the stature of the powerful men of the
world. . . . and creates its own ground for dissent in this world."

22. There is no doubt that Pharaoh is a historically identifiable agent.
Nonetheless the narrative is appropriated in new circumstances
because the narrative with historical reference is cast in terms of mythic
power. Thus in Psalms 87:4 and 89:10 Egypt and Pharaoh are referred
to by the mythical reference, Rahab. Frank M. Cross, *Canaanite Myth
and Hebrew Epic* (Cambridge: Harvard University, 1973) 77–144, has
shown how these elements are intertwined in the language.

23. Gottwald, *The Tribes of Yahweh,* chapter 55, has shown how Yahweh
is a function of a socioeconomic revolution. Nonetheless, as Gottwald
(697) affirms, Yahweh is understood as an identifiable agent.

24. Stanley Hauerwas, *A Community of Character* (Notre Dame:
University of Notre Dame, 1981), in a rather remarkable way shows
how story can maintain a world apart from the dominant system. See
also his programmatic statement, "From System to Story: An
Alternative Pattern for Rationality in Ethics," *Truthfulness and
Tragedy* (Notre Dame: University of Notre Dame, 1977) 15–39. See
the more recent comment of Hauerwas, "The Gesture of a Truthful
Story," *Theology Today* 42 (1985) 181–89.

25. Hans Walter Wolff, "Das Zitat im Prophetenspruch," *Gesammelte
Studien zum Alten Testament* (ThB 22: München: Chr. Kaiser Verlag,
1964) 36–129, has shown this pervasive device of the prophetic
literature.

26. George E. Mendenhall, "The Shady Side of Wisdom: The Date and
Purpose of Genesis 3," *A Light unto My Path,* ed. Howard N. Bream,
Ralph D. Heim, and Carey A. Moore (Philadelphia: Temple
University, 1974) 319–34, has shown how the "wise men" of the crown
help maintain the epistemological monopoly and therefore the royal
legitimacy. The Exodus narrative is aimed precisely against such a
monopoly of knowledge.

27. Practical evidence of such courage and imagination for the construction of countersystems of reality is evidenced in the work of the Oregon
Caring Skills Project in Eugene. Its director, George D. Parsons, gives
the following report in a private communication: the Project "teaches
children to be more caring in their daily lives using a rehearsal format
in which students practice delivering caring 'lines' in hypothetical
situations. In one public elementary school a group of fourth graders,
in a successful attempt to end the practice of humiliating students who

accidentally drop a food tray in the cafeteria, learned to say, 'I would like it if you would stop laughing at her.' These students were able, after intense rehearsal, to speak their lines with conviction when their peers made fun of an unfortunate student—and thus eliminated an abusive tradition at their school." George Parsons and his colleagues with the Project believe that all caring acts require a performance and that young people can be prepared to lead more caring lives by learning a new set of lines, a language of caring, that is alien to our society.

28. On this offer to every member of the community in the shaping of an alternative imagination, see Deuteronomy 29:10–11.

29. Genovese, *Roll, Jordan, Roll,* credits liturgic life, with the Black preacher and the Black mammy, as responsible for keeping the white world in the process of deconstruction and preventing its gaining legitimacy. On p. 360, he writes of this mammy, "And in her own way Mammy defended Black dignity."

30. On the symbiotic and deathly relation between oppressor and victim as it is acted out in social reality, see John Gaventa, *Power and Powerlessness: Quiescence and Rebellion in an Appalachian Valley* (Urbana: University of Illinois, 1980).

31. For an example of liturgy as assault, see *Minjung Theology,* ed. Kim Yong Bock (Singapore: The Christian Conference of Asia, 1981). This is a study of people's theology in Korea and its function in the face of a totalitarian regime.

32. On the social outcry as a public act of legitimation, see Brueggemann, "A Shape for Old Testament Theology, II: Embrace of Pain," *CBQ* 47 (1985) 395–415. See also Frank A. Spina, "The Concept of Social Rage in the Old Testament and the Ancient Near East" (Unpublished Dissertation, University of Michigan, 1977).

33. On "withdrawal" as a social strategy, see George Mendenhall, "The Hebrew Conquest of Palestine," *BAR* 3 (1970) 105–7, and Gottwald, *The Tribes of Yahweh,* 326, 408, and n. 326.

34. The phrase is from Peter L. Berger, *The Sacred Canopy* (Garden City, NY: Doubleday, 1967). Berger discusses the reality of withdrawal from the norms when those norms are incongruous with life experience.

35. Jon Gunnemann, *The Moral Meaning of Revolution* (New Haven: Yale University, 1979), has shown that the problem of theodicy is not simply a theological or moral problem, but it is a sociological problem when the social "rules of the game" are seen to be fundamentally unfair, even when legitimated by ideology. Thus revolution of a serious kind is an effort to change the settlement of social payoffs, which is a functional theodicy. See especially chapter 2 of Gunnemann's analysis.

36. Gottwald, *The Tribes of Yahweh,* in making Yahweh largely a "function" of the social experiment of Israel as a liberated community,

has closely tied together the identity of Yahweh and the identity of Israel. He has put the claims of covenant to an intense political use. In his study of Deuteronomic theology, Robert Polzin, *Moses and the Deuteronomist* (New York: Seabury, 1980) 37–38 and passim, has considered the interrelatedness of the uniqueness of Yahweh, the uniqueness of Israel, and the uniqueness of Moses. In some way, serious faith formation must articulate a uniqueness, or there is no identity, for identity is being able to distinguish who is "me" and who is "not me." That claim of uniqueness can also claim too much, as Polzin shows, and must be subjected to criticism.

37. Dale Patrick, *The Rendering of God in the Old Testament* (Philadelphia: Fortress, 1981), has done a careful delineation of what it means to present Yahweh as a character in the story. While it is more sophisticated in this regard, he follows the line of G. Ernest Wright in showing that Yahweh as a God cannot be separated from the recital of this story. In another way Sallie McFague, *Metaphorical Theology* (Philadelphia: Fortress, 1982), has also shown how God is rendered in the parables as a real referent, but as a referent known only inside the story.

38. On lament as an act of hope, see Erhard Gerstenberger, "Der klagende Mensch," *Probleme biblischer Theologie,* ed. Hans Walter Wolff (München: Chr. Kaiser Verlag, 1971) 64–72.

39. Dorothy Sölle, *The Strength of the Weak* (Philadelphia: Westminster, 1984), has proposed that all faithful feminist theology begins in pain. While that is surely true for feminist theology, one may extrapolate to say it is true of all faithful theology. It is equally true that our clue to this insight has come from feminist and other liberation movements in theology.

40. That ideology should cover over pain and keep it from visibility has close parallels to the analysis of R. D. Laing, *The Politics of Experience* (New York: Pantheon, 1967), who observes that in every political organization (including the family) *experience* is finally denied and covered over by approved *behavior.* What Laing treats in the family unit is treated broadly by the Old Testament. Experience includes awareness of oppression, and ideology defines the acceptable behavior which must deny the experience. The New Testament criticism of "law" can also be understood as ideology which denies the reality of human experience. On religious aspects of social behavior, see Marty E. Marty, *A Nation of Behavers* (Chicago: University of Chicago, 1976).

41. For the resilient power of the narrative in this regard, see Waltzer, *Exodus and Revolution.* The recent political effort of Jesse Jackson in American presidential politics is an example of appeal to this tradition. Every generation of oppressed people who appeal to this text can say with Moses and in concert with Jackson, "Our time has come."

42. In terms of historical realism this is of course an overstatement, but in the simplifying rhetoric of the text that is how the lines are drawn. Where imagination becomes private and autonomous, by that much one has ceased to be an Israelite.

43. See the carefully nuanced theological, hermeneutical comments of Bernhard W. Anderson on The Song of Miriam, "The Song of Miriam Poetically and Theologically Considered," forthcoming in JSOT Supplements, and my "Response" to Anderson in the same volume. See the poignant statement by Gail O'Day, "Singing Woman's Song: A Hermeneutic of Liberation," *CTM* 12 (1985) 203–10.

44. On the move from lament to doxology in the structure of the Exodus narrative, see James Plastaras, *The God of the Exodus* (Milwaukee: Bruce, 1966), especially chapter 3. On giving voice to experience in the Exodus event, see J. Severino Croatto, *Exodus: A Hermeneutic of Freedom* (Maryknoll NY: Orbis, 1981), especially chapters 2 and 4.

45. In a sense liturgic activity is "practice" for public action. In the example cited in n. 27, there was a precise rehearsal of lines prior to the public act. Perhaps such an insight suggests a particular reading of Mark 13:9–11.

46. Amos Wilder, *Theopoetic: Theology and the Religious Imagination* (Philadelphia: Fortress, 1976) 28. Wilder has extended this discussion of the battle for imagination in *Jesus' Parables and the War of the Myths: Essays on Imagination in the Scripture* (Philadelphia: Fortress, 1982).

47. Martin Buber, *Kingship of God* (New York: Harper & Row, 1967), first discerned that this is a serious political metaphor that should not be purged for the sake of religious expectations.

48. More than any other, George E. Mendenhall has explored the political intentionality of the covenant as the establishment of an alternative kingdom. See *Law and Covenant in Israel and the Ancient Near East* (Pittsburgh: Biblical Colloquium, 1955); *The Tenth Generation* (Baltimore: Johns Hopkins University, 1973) chapters 1, 7, 8; and "The Conflict Between Value Systems and Social Control," *Unity and Diversity*, ed. Hans Goedicke and J. J. M. Roberts (Baltimore: Johns Hopkins University, 1975) 169–80. His work should not be evaluated on the establishment of the Hittite parallels but on the basis of his insight into the political character of Israel's faith, shaped as it is by political metaphors.

49. It has remained for Norman Gottwald, *The Tribes of Yahweh*, to explore the concrete political implications of the covenant model. He has done this by arguing that Israel is not simply a religious community but a political, social experiment in justice and freedom. The radicalness of his political argument is suggested by his rather harsh verdict on Mendenhall (599–602). It is instructive that, at the most crucial place in his argument about the interface of politics and religion (697), Gottwald appeals precisely to Buber.

50. John Bright, *The Kingdom of God* (Nashville: Abingdon-Cokesbury, 1953), has provided a convenient summary of the function of the metaphor in biblical faith, though Gottwald, *The Tribes of Yahweh*, is likely correct in concluding that Bright has not adequately explored the radical political implications of this metaphor.
51. James Sanders, "Torah and Christ," *Interpretation* 29 (1975) 372–90, has suggested that torah has two aspects, ethos and ethics. I do not want to force his categories, but it occurs to me that these might be correlated, ethos as *liturgic practice* and ethics as *social implementation*. Clearly torah is not simply social implementation, for that could not be sustained without regular liturgic practice that keeps the social implementation credible and open. On tales of empowering imagination in the torah, see Brueggemann, "Passion and Perspective: Two Dimensions of Education in the Bible," *Theology Today* 42 (1985) 179.
52. On the foundational meaning of covenant for social life, see the acute analysis of John F. A. Taylor, *The Masks of Society* (New York: Appleton-Century-Crofts, 1966). His analysis adds important support for the suggestion of Lohfink in n. 54 concerning the social intentionality of Deuteronomy.
53. Gerhard von Rad, *Studies in Deuteronomy* (Chicago: Henry Regnery, 1953) chapters 1 and 5. See also *Old Testament Theology I* (New York: Harper & Brothers, 1962) 219–31. We have some distance to go to understand that torah is an activity of obedient imagination. See my statement, "Imagination as a Mode of Fidelity," *Understanding the Word: Festschrift* for Bernhard Anderson, ed. James T. Butler, Edgar W. Conrad, and Ben Ollenberger (JSOT Supp 37; Sheffield: University of Sheffield, 1985), 13–36.
54. Norbert Lohfink, *Great Themes from the Old Testament* (Chicago: Franciscan Herald, 1982) chapter 4, has proposed that in Deuteronomy 16—19 we are offered a "constitution" for Israel as an alternatively organized political entity. While this may be an overstatement, it is important to see that this is not a random collection of isolated rules, but there is present a governing notion of Israel as a different kind of political community.
55. Fernando Belo, *A Materialist Reading of the Gospel of Mark* (Maryknoll, NY: Orbis, 1981).
56. Paul D. Hanson, "The Theological Significance of Contradiction within the Book of the Covenant," *Canon and Authority*, ed. George W. Coats and Burke O. Long (Philadelphia: Fortress, 1977) 110–31, has shrewdly discerned that within the Book of the Covenant one can distinguish those elements of law which envision a liberated society and those which do not. It is possible to correlate Hanson's concrete analysis with Belo's construct of laws on *purity* and *debt cancellation*.

57. An obvious counterpoint to this statement is found in the royal traditions of creation and wisdom which are concerned for equilibrium, cosmic and social. On such equilibrium as a theological concern, see H. H. Schmid, *Gerechtigkeit als Weltordnung* (Tübingen: Mohr [Siebeck], 1968). See my comments on this theological concern in "A Shape for Old Testament Theology, I: Structure Legitimation," *CBQ* 47 (1985) 28–46.

Chapter 2

1. See the analysis of the Exodus narrative in these categories in "The Exodus Narrative as Israel's Articulation of Faith Development," chapter 1 above.
2. The theme is well summarized by Elizabeth Achtemeier, "Righteousness in the Old Testament," *IBD* (New York: Abingdon, 1962) 4.80–85. Note especially in her bibliography the dynamic approach of Pedersen, the theological approach of Eichrodt, the cultic approach of von Rad, and the juridical approach of Fahlgren. See also the accompanying article by Paul J. Achtemeier, "Righteousness in the New Testament," ibid., 91–99.
3. See the recent study of Christian ethics by James M. Gustafson, *Ethics from a Theocentric Perspective* (Chicago: University of Chicago, 1981), in which he takes a radically theocentric view, some believe almost to the loss of a Christian referent. In that regard he presses the point of his teacher, H. Richard Niebuhr, *Radical Monotheism and Western Culture* (New York: Harper & Row, 1960).
4. Kurt Galling, "Der Beichtspiegel," *ZAW* 47 (1929) 125–30. See the excellent study of this chapter by Georg Fohrer, "The Righteous Man in Job 31," *Essays in Old Testament Ethics*, ed. James L. Crenshaw (New York: KTAV, 1974) 1–22.
5. That metaphor can perhaps be translated in a variety of different ways. It would seem that the Johannine rendering is "eternal life." Obviously whenever it is translated the specifics of meaning are changed. For a nontheistic rendering I suggest that is the import of Jürgen Habermas, *Legitimation Crisis* (Boston: Beacon, 1975) 105, where he speaks of a "communication community" and an ideal speech situation. See Fowler's exploration of the power of the metaphor for H. Richard Niebuhr, *To See the Kingdom* (New York: Abingdon, 1974).
6. Paul D. Hanson, *The Dawn of Apocalyptic* (Philadelphia: Fortress, 1975).
7. Elizabeth Achtemeier, *The Community and Message of Isaiah 56—66* (Minneapolis: Augsburg, 1982).

8. Brevard S. Childs, *Introduction to the Old Testament as Scripture* (Philadelphia: Fortress, 1979) 325–38.

9. Ronald E. Clements, "The Unity of the Book of Isaiah," *Interpretation* 36 (1982) 117–29, and "Beyond Tradition-History: Deutero-Isaianic Development of First Isaiah's Themes," *JSOT* 31 (1985) 95–113.

10. Ronald E. Clements, "Patterns in the Prophetic Canon," *Canon and Authority*, ed. George W. Coats and Burke O. Long (Philadelphia: Fortress, 1977) 42–55, has observed this as a general tendency in the formation of the prophetic literature.

11. For the critical basis of these categories in the book of Isaiah, see Brueggemann, "Unity and Dynamic in the Isaiah Tradition," *JSOT* 29 (1984) 89–107.

12. The clearest articulation of "righteousness" as power for life has been made by Klaus Koch, *The Prophets: The Assyrian Period* (Philadelphia: Fortress, 1982) 56–62. This brief comment derives from Koch's important study on the "destiny-fulfilling power" of deeds, a hypothesis that has not gone unchallenged.

13. H. H. Schmid, "Schöpfung, Gerechtigkeit und Heil: Schöpfungstheologie als Gesamthorizont biblischer Theologie," *ZTK* 70 (1973) 1–19, and *Gerechtigkeit als Weltordnung* (Tübingen: Mohr [Siebeck], 1968), has shown how righteousness is Yahweh's way of ordaining order in creation. Violation of that order leads to death. The "woe oracles" of Isaiah 5:8–23; 10:1–4 likely reflect that notion of righteousness.

14. On the word pair in the prophets, see Reinhard Fey, *Amos und Jesaja: Abhängigkeit und Eigenständigkeit des Jesaja* (WMANT 12; Neukirchen-Vluyn: Neukirchener Verlag, 1963) 24–56, and Hans Walter Wolff, *Amos the Prophet* (Philadelphia: Fortress, 1973) 59–67. Fey's general hypothesis has not been well received, but his evidence on this particular theme is worth considering.

15. See the poignant utilization of this metaphor by Robert Jewett, "A Covenant with Death," *Christian Century* 100 (1983) 477–78.

16. On the dynamic relation of life and righteousness, see Gerhard von Rad, " 'Righteousness' and 'Life' in the Cultic Language of the Psalms," *The Problem of the Hexateuch and Other Essays* (New York: McGraw-Hill, 1966) 243–66.

17. Koch's dynamic understanding of the term lets us move from a notion of *norm* to one of salvific *power*. The righteousness which saves is one which supersedes and overcomes the righteousness of moral obedience.

18. The pursuit of what is "right," in a juridical context, is not unlike the question of Pilate (John 18:38) in which it is clear that the old norms of what is true have failed. See the comments of Paul Lehmann, *The Transfiguration of Politics* (New York: Harper & Row, 1975) 59 and passim, where he contrasts "truth-power" with "state-power." What is

presented in the Fourth Gospel is already at issue in Second Isaiah around the question of what is righteous.

19. On the use of the creation traditions in Second Isaiah, see Carroll Stuhlmueller, *Creative Redemption in Deutero-Isaiah* (Analecta Biblica 43; Rome: Biblical Institute, 1980); Rainer Albertz, *Weltschöpfung und Menschenschöpfung* (Calwer Theologische Monographien 3; Stuttgart: Calwer Verlag, 1974); and Rolf Rendtorff, "Die theologische Stellung des Schöpfungsglaubens bei Deuterojesaja," *ZTK* 51 (1954) 3–13.

20. Hanson, *The Dawn of Apocalyptic*, 201, explores the ironic dimension of this poem.

21. Herbert Donner, "Jesaja lvi 1–7: Ein Abrogationsfall innerhalb des Kanons—Implikationen und Konsequenzen," *STV* 36 (1985) 81–95, has shown how this text is a direct and intentional abrogation of the old torah teaching of Deuteronomy 23:1–8.

22. An important connection must be discerned between imagination and land redistribution. Indeed the most radical imaginative act of these texts is to be able to position an alternative way of thinking about the land. The radical vision of redistribution stands in contrast with our conventional view of land which imagines that it must be the way it is. The root text is the Jubilee year in Leviticus 25. See also Micah 2:1–5; Mark 10:17–31; and the analysis of theories of land tenure by Robert Coote, *Amos Among the Prophets* (Philadelphia: Fortress, 1981) 24–32. The radical implications for *social organization* flow precisely from a *liberated imagination*.

23. A case can be made that it is especially loss of "turf" which causes lamentation; and in turn such honest lamentation must lead to free imagination that can think freshly about land.

24. This text no doubt has reference to the metaphor (and institution?) of Jubilee in Leviticus 25. The future of this imaginative text is evident in Luke 4:18–19. See James A. Sanders, "Isaiah in Luke," *Interpretation* 36 (1982) 144–55, especially p. 151, and Sharon Ringe, *Jesus, Liberation, and the Jubilee Year*, (Philadelphia: Fortress, 1985).

25. There are surely important links between this text and 1:21–26. Isaiah 1 is likely to be seen, as Fohrer and Childs have urged, as a programmatic statement which anticipates the entire book of Isaiah. If so, then 65:17–25 is completing the "afterward" of 1:26.

26. This theme of the "oaks" which practice the "new righteousness" of liberation may be a way to hold a variety of biblical themes together. On the one hand, it may look back to Psalm 1, where the torah keepers are the resilient trees. At the beginning of the Isaiah tradition (1:30) the use of oaks is closely paralleled to the use in Psalm 1:3. On the other hand, it is in Romans 8:21 that the new children of God are transformed (12:2) for the new righteousness.

Chapter 3

1. A good example of this is the several generations of Black American baseball players. They were not permitted in the "Major" leagues. The Black baseball leagues had an impressive standard of baseball itself, but it was not noticed, and of course the records set in that league are "nonrecords." See Jules Tygiel, *Baseball's Great Experiment* (New York: Oxford University, 1983), for a full discussion.
2. Gerhard von Rad, "The Form-Critical Problem of the Hexateuch," *The Problem of the Hexateuch and Other Essays* (New York: McGraw-Hill, 1966); *Old Testament Theology I* (New York: Harper & Row, 1962); and pervasively in his work.
3. George Ernest Wright, *God Who Acts* (SBT 8; London: SCM, 1952); *The Old Testament and Theology* (New York: Harper & Row, 1969).
4. James Barr, "Revelation through History in the Old Testament and in Modern Theology," *Interpretation* 17 (1963) 193–205; "The Old Testament and the New Crisis of Biblical Authority," *Interpretation* 25 (1971) 24–40; "Story and History in Biblical Theology," *JR* 56 (1976) 1–17. Barr has extended his critique in a variety of places; see *The Scope and Authority of the Bible* (Explorations in Theology 7; London: SCM, 1980).
5. See especially Brevard S. Childs, *Biblical Theology in Crisis* (Philadelphia: Westminster, 1970), for his most incisive statement. Childs continues to offer a constructive alternative in *Introduction to the Old Testament as Scripture* (Philadelphia: Fortress, 1979).
6. The shift methodologically from historical to literary studies is an evidence of the problematic now faced by scholars. On this shift see the summary by Robert Polzin, *Moses and the Deuteronomist* (New York: Seabury, 1980) chapter 1. The problem revolves around a false claim of objectivity which cannot be sustained and of which the methods of criticism have been largely unaware. See the programmatic statement of J. G. Davies, "Subjectivity and Objectivity in Biblical Exegesis," *BJRL* 66 (1983) 44–53.
7. Concerning Jeremiah there is of course some dispute whether the beginning of his ministry is in 626 or 609. The earlier date is conventional but Holliday, following Hyatt, holds to the later date. Robert Carroll regards such a question as irrelevant to the material and does not try to link the text so precisely to historical context.
8. Bernhard W. Anderson, *Understanding the Old Testament* (3rd ed.; Englewood Cliffs, NJ: Prentice-Hall, 1975); John Bright, *A History of Israel* (3rd ed., Philadelphia: Westminster, 1981); Martin Noth, *The History of Israel* (New York: Harper & Brothers, 1958); Siegfried Herrmann, *A History of Israel in Old Testament Times* (Philadelphia: Fortress, 1981).

9. See my argument in more detail on this point in *1 Kings, 2 Kings* (Atlanta: John Knox, 1982).
10. Robert Wilson, *Prophecy and Society in Ancient Israel* (Philadelphia: Fortress, 1980), shows how many of the prophets are "peripheral," i.e., voices who speak for those who have become marginal in society. On the prophets and the marginal, see Robert Coote, *Amos Among the Prophets* (Philadelphia: Fortress, 1981), and Hans Walter Wolff, "Micah the Moreshite—The Prophet and His Background," *Israelite Wisdom*, ed. John G. Gammie (Missoula, MT: Scholars, 1978) 77–84.
11. On prophetic word becoming historical event, see von Rad, *Studies in Deuteronomy* (Chicago: Henry Regnery, 1953) chapter 7.
12. On Jeremiah's alternative perception of reality, see Brueggemann, "The Epistemological Crisis of Israel's Two Histories (Jer. 9:22–23)" *Israelite Wisdom*, ed. John G. Gammie, 85–105.
13. See most recently Peter R. Ackroyd, "The Book of Jeremiah—Some Recent Studies," *JSOT* 28 (1984) 47–59. However, even if one takes such a minimalist view, one must nonetheless deal with the portrayal of the person given in the text. On this portrayal, see Brueggemann, "The Book of Jeremiah: Portrait of the Prophet," *Interpretation* 37 (1983) 130–45.
14. On the question of theodicy, see the splendid resource collection edited by James L. Crenshaw, *Theodicy in the Old Testament* (Philadelphia: Fortress, 1983).
15. On the complaints, see von Rad, "The Confessions of Jeremiah," *Theodicy in the Old Testament*, ed. James L. Crenshaw, 88–99, and the more recent literature cited by Norbert Ittmann, *Die Konfessionen Jeremias* (WMANT 54; Neukirchen-Vluyn: Neukirchener Verlag, 1981).
16. Robert Cushman, *Faith Seeking Understanding* (Durham, NC: Duke University, 1980) xi–xv.
17. On these images, see James Muilenburg, "The Terminology of Adversity in Jeremiah," *Translating and Understanding the Old Testament*, ed. Harry Thomas Frank and William L. Reed (New York: Abingdon, 1970) 42–63.
18. See Werner E. Lemke, "The Near and the Distant God: A Study of Jer. 23:23–24 in Its Biblical Theological Context," *JBL* 100 (1981) 541–55.
19. On the social function of idols, see *The Idols of Death and the God of Life*, ed. Pablo Richard (Maryknoll, NY: Orbis, 1983). It is clear, as has now been suggested by various authors, that the modern problem, as indeed the ancient problem, is not atheism but idolatry.
20. Bernhard Lang, "The Social Organization of Peasant Poverty in Biblical Israel," *JSOT* 24 (1982) 47–63.
21. See n. 10.

22. See n. 10.
23. See Henri Mottu, "Jeremiah vs. Hananiah: Ideology and Truth in Old Testament Prophecy," *The Bible and Liberation*, ed. Norman K. Gottwald (Maryknoll, N.Y.: Orbis, 1983) 235–51.
24. On this text, see José Miranda, *Marx and the Bible* (Maryknoll, NY: Orbis, 1974) 44–53. For biblical interpretation which concerns these issues, see the important collection *God of the Lowly*, ed. Willy Schottroff and Wolfgang Stegemann (Maryknoll, NY: Orbis, 1984).
25. Exactly how hope and judgment are to be assigned in the tradition of Jeremiah is difficult. Certainly Nicholson and Carroll are correct in their judgment that much of the hope literature is exilic and after Jeremiah. Yet it seems highly probable to me that the roots of hope in the tradition are found in the person of Jeremiah. Not all of it can systematically be assigned to the Deuteronomic redactors and traditionists.
26. This is the inclination of Robert Carroll, *From Chaos to Covenant* (New York: Crossroad, 1981) 202 and passim.
27. Isaiah 54:7–8 is an important text for the claim that there is continuity *through* the chaos. However, it is clear that this text, commonly dated 540, is a later rereading of the situation. The rereading later on permits such an affirmation, but such a reading earlier in the midst of the chaos (as with Hananiah) would be a false reading. The rereading of Second Isaiah must not be permitted to nullify the more drastic reading of Jeremiah in the context of the crisis itself.
28. On the dramatic, rhetorical ground of the new social possibility, see Thomas M. Raitt, *A Theology of Exile* (Philadelphia: Fortress, 1977), especially chapters 5 and 6.
29. It is unclear whether the exiled community was "the poor." The usual assumption is that the poor were left behind, but see Jeremiah 52:15. In any case, whether poor or not, they were certainly marginal and devalued in their new cultural setting. See my discussion of Jeremiah 24, "A Second Reading of Jeremiah After the Dismantling," *Ex Auditu* 1 (1985) 156–68.
30. That God chooses the rejected as the wave of the future is poignantly articulated in the metaphor of the rejected stone being made the cornerstone (cf. 1 Peter 2:7). For the purposes of this essay, it is important to read that metaphor not only christologically but also sociologically. For such a sociology, see John Elliott, *A Home for the Homeless* (Philadelphia: Fortress, 1981).
31. Such a view is against the common reading of the historical process. For a sense of history-making done by power agents (as the world judges power), see the splendid statement by Andrew B. Schmookler, *The Parable of the Tribes* (Berkeley: University of California, 1984). On p. 61 he states his thesis, "History is shaped by the powerful." But

that leaves unanswered the decisive question, "What finally consti-
tutes power?" (on which see 1 Cor. 1:18–25).
32. See especially George E. Mendenhall, "The Shady Side of Wisdom:
The Date and Purpose of Genesis 3," *A Light unto My Path*, ed.
Howard N. Bream, Ralph D. Heim, and Carey A. Moore
(Philadelphia: Temple University, 1974) 319–34. Mendenhall's presentation of wisdom teachers suggests they intend to stop the historical
process.
33. Carlos Fuentes, "High Noon in Latin America," *Vanity Fair* 46, no. 7
(September, 1983) 43–51.
34. Ibid., 47.
35. Ibid., 51.
36. After completion of this chapter, I had occasion to read J. Anthony
Lukas, *Common Ground* (New York: Alfred A. Knopf, 1985), a
detailed analysis of the Boston crisis over the integration of public
schools. Among the central figures in the crisis was Louise Day Hicks,
who increasingly became a key voice of resistance to social integration.
In his attempt to characterize Hicks' role in the crisis, Lukas (129)
writes:

> Ruth Batson once cornered her in a classroom and, shaking a finger
> at her, shouted, "You had an opportunity to change history. Instead
> history is going to record you as the woman who impeded history."
> A whole generation of children has been lost because of Louise
> Hicks.

The categories of "change-impede" used by Batson correlate precisely
with my analysis of history-making and history-stopping. Hicks is a
clear embodiment of the negative side of my argument.

Chapter 4

1. Gerhard von Rad, *Old Testament Theology I* (New York: Harper &
Row, 1962) 165–75. That the patriarchal narratives focus on hope is,
of course, the main interpretive point of his Genesis commentary as
well.
2. Claus Westermann, *The Promise to the Fathers* (Philadelphia:
Fortress, 1980).
3. David J. A. Clines, *The Theme of the Pentateuch* (JSOT Supp 10;
Sheffield: University of Sheffield, 1978) 31–43, has helpfully
summarized and categorized the data.
4. Albrecht Alt, "The God of the Fathers," *Essays on Old Testament
History and Religion* (Oxford: Blackwell, 1966) 1–66.

124   HOPE WITHIN HISTORY

5. Paul Ricoeur, "Guilt, Ethics and Religion," *The Conflict of Interpretations* (Evanston: Northwestern University, 1974) 436–39. For the classic statement of Jürgen Moltmann, see *Theology of Hope* (New York: Harper & Row, 1967) chapter 2, on the distinction of promise and epiphany.

6. See the analysis of Hans Walter Wolff, "The Kerygma of the Yahwist," *The Vitality of Old Testament Traditions,* ed. Walter Brueggemann and Hans Walter Wolff (2nd ed; Atlanta: John Knox, 1982) 46–55.

7. On the theological function of this narrative, see Brueggemann, " 'Impossibility' and Epistemology in the Faith Tradition of Abraham and Sarah (Gen. 18:1–15)," *ZAW* 94 (1982) 615–34.

8. Von Rad, *Old Testament Theology II* (New York: Harper & Row, 1965), has considered these matters in detail. See especially 263–77 on the new dimensions of prophetic hope in the sixth century.

9. See my discussion of the text, " 'Vine and Fig Tree': A Case Study in Imagination and Criticism," *CBQ* 43 (1981) 188–204.

10. See the argument of Hans Walter Wolff, "Micah the Moreshite—The Prophet and His Background," *Israelite Wisdom,* ed. John G. Gammie (Missoula, MT: Scholars, 1979) 77–84. By his close attention to the text Wolff has offered important support to the more general sociological perspective of American scholars.

11. On this passage see the analysis of Norman K. Gottwald, *All the Kingdoms of the Earth* (New York: Harper & Row, 1964) 222–28. More generally on prophetic promises, see Thomas M. Raitt, *A Theology of Exile* (Philadelphia: Fortress, 1977).

12. That is the normal argument of scholars. See especially Paul D. Hanson, *The Dawn of Apocalyptic* (Philadelphia: Fortress, 1975). A minority opinion is held by Gerhard von Rad, *Old Testament Theology II*, 301–8. See the review of various positions in the collection edited by Paul D. Hanson, *Visionaries and Their Apocalypses* (Philadelphia: Fortress, 1983).

13. See Michael Stone, *Scriptures, Sects and Visions* (Philadelphia: Fortress, 1980).

14. Martin Buber, *Kingship of God* (New York: Harper & Row, 1967), has seen this at the beginning of the current scholarly discussion. That is, the "kingdom" emerging out of Sinai was not simply a religious movement, but a political alternative in the world in which the category of obedience was decisive. Buber's work anticipated the later developments of Mendenhall and Gottwald. Buber's understanding at a very early time gave him a peculiarly critical posture over against political Zionism.

15. Sallie McFague, *Metaphorical Theology* (Philadelphia: Fortress, 1982), has shown how the metaphor of "kingdom of God" became

crucial for the faith and literature of the faith community. The metaphor is at work in the parables of Jesus as in the apocalypse, both of which are forms of imaginative, subversive literature.

16. On a radical reading of the prayer, see Michael Crosby, *Thy Will Be Done: Our Father as Subversive Activity* (Maryknoll, NY: Orbis, 1977). Sharon H. Ringe, *Jesus, Liberation, and the Biblical Jubilee* (Philadelphia: Fortress, 1985), shows how the Lord's Prayer is linked to the social hope of the Jubilee year which, of course, then has important political and economic implications.

17. On a most helpful proposal for penetrating to the common core of tradition and faith, see Paul van Buren, *Discerning the Way* (New York: Seabury, 1980). See also Marcus Barth, *The People of God* (JSNT Supp. 5; Sheffield: JSOT, 1983) 25–26 and passim.

18. See the basic study of Richard R. Niebuhr, *Resurrection and Historical Reason* (New York: Scribner, 1957), and the programmatic essay of W. B. Gallie, "The Historical Understanding," *History and Theory*, ed. George H. Nadel (Middletown, CT: Wesleyan University, 1977) 149–202, on the theological method required by narrative.

19. Jürgen Moltmann has attempted to deal with this interface in his book *Hope and Planning* (New York: Harper & Row, 1971).

20. On relinquishment as an act of faith, see Marie Augusta Neal, *A Socio-Theology of Letting Go* (New York: Paulist, 1977).

21. See Moltmann, *Hope and Planning,* and M. Douglas Meeks, *Origins of the Theology of Hope* (Philadelphia: Fortress, 1974).

22. For such extrapolations, see the popular statement of John Naisbitt, *Megatrends: Ten New Directions Transforming Our Lives* (New York: Warner, 1982). The book warrants serious criticism for having bracketed out all of the human questions. Such a way of scientific extrapolation tends to be positivistic and without reference to the realities of social criticism. As such, its most likely function is not *descriptive* but is a part of the *ideological* argument.

23. The slogan "the system is the solution" was invented by a phone company official for whom the company is indeed the solution. The slogan was not devised by an irate phone user who each month gets a mistaken computerized bill for $673 and cannot get it corrected.

24. See my book entitled *Living Toward a Vision* (Philadelphia: United Church, 1976), from which the title of this chapter is taken.

25. On "delegitimation" and social withdrawal of authority, see George E. Mendenhall, "The Hebrew Conquest of Palestine," *The Biblical Archaeologist Reader 3,* ed. Eward F. Campbell, Jr. and David Noel Freedman (Garden City, NY: Doubleday, 1970) 100–120, and the derivations made from that social act by Norman K. Gottwald, *The Tribes of Yahweh* (Maryknoll, NY: Orbis, 1979) 408–9 and passim.

John Swomley, *Liberation Ethics* (New York: Macmillan, 1972), has suggested how delegitimation and withdrawal function in the actual practice of radical ethics.

26. On the cruciality of imagination for liberation, see Frederick Herzog, "Liberation and Imagination," *Interpretation* 32 (1978) 227–41. Paul Ricoeur, in many of his writings, has understood the power of liberated imagination. See a succinct statement, "Philosophical Hermeneutics and Biblical Hermeneutics," *Exegesis: Problems and Method and Exercises in Reading (Genesis 22 and Luke 15),* ed. François Bovon and Gregoire Rouiller (Pittsburgh Theological Monograph Series 21; Pittsburgh: Pickwick, 1978) 321–39.

27. See Paul D. Hanson, *The Dawn of Apocalyptic,* and, derivatively, Elizabeth Achtemeier, *The Community and Message of Isaiah 56—66* (Minneapolis: Augsburg, 1982).

28. On the political and symbolic futurity of the Daniel–Nebuchadnezzar literature, see W. Sibley Towner, "Were the English Puritans 'the Saints of the Most High?' " *Interpretation* 37 (1983) 46–63.

29. Herbert N. Schneidau, *Sacred Discontent: The Bible and Western Tradition* (Baton Rouge: Louisiana State University, 1977).

30. On the ideological containment of such intellectuals in the ancient world, see George E. Mendenhall, "The Shady Side of Wisdom: The Date and Purpose of Genesis 3," *A Light unto My Path,* ed. Howard N. Bream, Ralph D. Heim, and Carey A. Moore (Philadelphia: Temple University, 1974) 319–34, and, less directly, Glendon E. Bryce, *A Legacy of Wisdom* (Lewisburg: Bucknell University, 1979), especially chapters 7 and 8.

31. Von Rad, *Old Testament Theology I,* 438–41, has noted six proverbs that speak against human control and with respect to the inscrutable mystery by which God governs. That, however, is against the main inclination of this literature. See also von Rad, *Wisdom in Israel* (Nashville: Abingdon, 1972) 98–110.

32. In addition to the writings of Mendenhall and Bryce cited in n. 30, see Robert Gordis, *Poets, Prophets and Sages* (Bloomington: Indiana University, 1971) 160–97, and Brian W. Kovacs, "Is There a Class-Ethic in Proverbs?" *Essays in Old Testament Ethics,* ed. James L. Crenshaw and John T. Willis (New York: KTAV, 1974) 171–89.

33. On the capacity of civility to effect social control and oppression, see Norbert Elias, *Power and Civility* (New York: Pantheon, 1982), and John M. Cuddihy, *The Ordeal of Civility* (New York: Basic, 1974).

34. See David Halberstam, *The Best and the Brightest* (New York: Random House, 1972). Those who served the government's effort in the Vietnam War were certainly not lacking in intelligence, but it became intelligence in the service of uncriticized power. The same thing happened with the agents of the Watergate cover-up. Reason

that is contained uncriticized in the system is likely to be ideological, self-serving, and, finally, oppressive.

Chapter 5

1. John Westerhoff, III, *Will Our Children Have Faith?* (New York: Seabury, 1976).
2. On the crisis of finding an adequate language, see Herbert Marcuse, *One-Dimensional Man* (Boston: Beacon, 1964) chapter 4.
3. On this text I am especially helped and moved by the comments of Emil Fackenheim, "New Hearts and Old Covenant: On Some Possibilities of a Fraternal Jewish-Christian Reading of the Jewish Bible Today," *The Divine Helmsman*, ed. James L. Crenshaw and Samuel Sandmel (New York: KTAV, 1980) 191–205. See also Abraham J. Heschel, *The Prophets* (New York: Harper & Row, 1962) chapters 6, 12, and 14, and K. Kitamori, *Theology of the Pain of God* (Atlanta: John Knox, 1965).
4. Such pseudoforms of evangelical faith may appear both in secular fascinations with "passages" which know too much about the outcome and in religious certitudes that promise too much too soon and without real risk or pain.
5. The connections between Jeremiah and Job on critical grounds are sufficient warrant to draw an imaginative link between the two literatures.
6. Peter R. Ackroyd, "Continuity and Discontinuity: Rehabilitation and Authentication," *Tradition and Theology in the Old Testament*, ed. Douglas A. Knight (Philadelphia: Fortress, 1977) 215–34, has pointed to the resilient ways in which the community of faith struggles for continuity in the face of the painful and real discontinuities of experience.
7. I am grateful to my student Keven Andrews, who called my attention to these precise parallels.
8. See George A. Benson, *Then Joy Breaks Through* (New York: Seabury, 1972). Of course Benson does not suggest that the mere passage of time will resolve matters, for suppressed hurt endures with power. But Benson does reflect on the reality of a bottoming that is reached on occasions of unflinching candor.
9. On the distinctive theological contribution of Lamentations, see Norman K. Gottwald, *Studies in the Book of Lamentations* (Chicago: Alec R. Allenson, 1954). As Gottwald sees it, the bottom is reached in Lamentations in a way consonant with Benson's suggestions, i.e., through genuine candor and pain.

10. The dialectic of Jeremiah and Second Isaiah is in decisive ways an anticipation of the dialectic of crucifixion/resurrection, which has been most clearly articulated by Jürgen Moltmann, especially in his two books on the two points of the dialectic, *Theology of Hope* and *The Crucified God*.

11. Elie Wiesel, "Talking and Writing and Keeping Silent," *The German Church Struggle and the Holocaust*, ed. Franklin H. Littell and Hubert G. Locke (Detroit: Wayne State University, 1974) 271–74. I am grateful to Robert McAfee Brown for this reference.

12. Alexander and Margarete Mitscherlich, *The Inability to Mourn* (New York: Grove, 1975). I was led to this analysis by Robert Lifton's work, but see also the use made of their work by Moltmann, *The Experiment Hope* (Philadelphia: Fortress, 1975) 158.

13. Robert Jay Lifton, *The Broken Connection* (New York: Simon and Schuster, 1979).

14. Ibid., 293–94.

15. Walker Percy, *The Message in the Bottle* (New York: Farrar, Straus and Giroux 1975) chapter 6.

16. See the thoughtful theological analysis of this turn-point by Langdon Gilkey, *Society and the Sacred: Toward a Theology of Culture in Decline* (New York: Crossroad, 1981). See also the shrewd argument of Carl A. Raschke, *The Bursting of New Wineskins* (Pittsburgh: Pickwick, 1978).